THE
LONG
CANOE

Malcolm A . Hoffmann

Library of Congress 94–68421
ISBN 1–57087–075–6

Distributed by Portage Publications, Inc.
12 East 41st Street
New York, NY 10017

Printed by Professional Press
Chapel Hill, NC 27515-4371

Contents

Acknowledgements

To my daughter, Dr. Jessica Davis, for the jacket to this book and for the pleasures of her many contributions to civilized life;

To my daughter, Dr. Gertrude Bolter, for reasons similar to the above;

To my dearest, Miriam Miller, Esq., for love in old age;

To Shelagh Hackett, Gwynne Tomlan and Janis Anderson for taking dictation with patience and affection;

To Mrs. Beatrice Cohart for proofreading;

To Cousin Jewel who loves and instructs us all;

To Joseph Rosenbaum, for his wise counseling;

To various photographers, mostly unknown, for help in keeping the past alive in this book;

And to those Americans who in the Twentieth Century have survived at least six armed conflicts with other nations, three economic depressions, five epidemics and the breakdown of marriage, courage, integrity and such conduct as we used to call virtue. If genocide has been reestablished in the last decade and famine and plague are killing more now than ever, we shall leave the Twentieth Century with the computer as our conqueror. We couldn't shape the bytes for virtue.

I thank you for sharing the century with me and creating the illusion of a triumph of western civilization. But, still the hope that Prometheus gave us persists: It will be better in the Twenty First Century.

Introduction

Among the exciting myths of our culture is the story of Prometheus everlastingly bound to the rock because he brought fire to earth in defiance of the gods. Zeus, however, punished Prometheus not only for giving man bright-faced fire, but also because he caused mortals to cease foreseeing doom. When asked what cure he provided them with against this sickness, Prometheus replied, "I placed in them mine hopes." It may be that was the more important reason for the torturing of Prometheus, that hope was a more significant gift to man than fire.

All my life, I have preserved an optimist's modality of thought against terrible opposition. I have long held to the view that where the data is obscure, where rational men can differ sensibly as to the meaning to be drawn from facts, rational man should affirm the more optimistic inference.

I have often boldly called myself an optimist and, indeed, hold that I am one. Such optimism as mine is not glandular, was not born out of a succession of lucky events, nor a continued life of important accomplishments, nor a never-failing sense of well-being. I have known the deaths of all my immediate family, save my children, and defeats and frustrations which I did not always bear gracefully; I often have had the feeling of fighting battles with my hands tied behind my back. But I am, at 81 years of age, an optimist because I recognize that I learn from experience, that I have loved and still love, that my past equips me for tomorrow. My hand held my beloved's hand as she died, the wife I put above all the world, and yet I have lived to love again. For more than half a century I have practiced law in the United States and in the State of New York and a few foreign countries, and now, when the hounds of death are biting, I shall return again to writing.

If the gods had as much wisdom about men as men have about themselves, they would provide a second youth for older men, at least as an earned reward for goodness on earth. So thought Euripides. Instead, in our culture old people are placed in procrustean beds, and shaped to fit what others think should be done with them. You, of course, remember Procrustes, the innkeeper with the long bed on which he put short travellers, and the short bed on which he placed long. During the night he stretched the short ones on a rack, or with a yank amputated the long legs. The old just don't fit. They increase rapidly in number, but rapidly lose prestige and standing in society.

There has been a balance of levels of ages in the last centuries now upset, which thinned the number of men who would arrive at the fullness of years. The colander of life shook through only a few hardy survivors with the possible result that being rare they were revered. In much of Africa today, the life expectancy for the male is under age 30. In Gabon, life expectancy for the male is only 25 years in contrast with Iceland where it is 71. At the time of the Constitutional Convention, the fathers averaged about age 40, although there were some wise old ones present and accounted for. The relationship between the aged and the young has been disturbed by many things including tetracycline, cortisone, and just plain soap. Professor Dennis Gabor in his book "INVENTING THE FUTURE" points out that the British nanny did irreparable harm to India, more so than the British troops, by bringing to India soap and the institution of washing. Soap led many children who normally would be stricken by native bacteria and downed before coming of age to live to a fullness of years providing more mouths for feeding and causing widespread starvation. The United States, however, has been so affluent that it not only supported young people on welfare, or in the universities, but it also extended social security benefit to the aged whether they needed it or not.

I have had an enduring love affair with this country, not likely to end in my lifetime, no matter how far the politicians go to trivialize the romance, and the office seekers to dissonate its song

Now, at the end of the Century, the optimist's view shifts to survival for the group rather than the individual. Prometheus brought us fire. The fire has no limitation in its use. It can heat cold buildings and cook food. It can temper iron into steel and activate inert molecules, but it can also burn life away, a continent or even a planet at a time. And, its unleashed powers can make fools and cowards of us all. When Prometheus brought hope it necessarily included the hope that man could survive his use of fire, and perhaps one day in some pleasanter form enjoy the use of fire because its mischievousness has been abated.

Sometimes the community called earth protects itself from destruction as when small islands are found far from big ones, and in deep water, all in a stream of bacteria, which changes its form in order to overcome a combative fungus. But, the most destructive battle of all which nature provides for mankind is man's war with himself, a never ending struggle, between Sohrab and Rustum, in which the loser is always the same unpurposeful collection of chromosomes and other bits of matter for making human beings that in a few eons inevitably must be replaced by others who seemingly are pushing forward to some new level of human dignity. It is here on a long segment of contiguous sea, where the optimist can lay his hopes.

Rain forest and sub-tropical islands everywhere make such a show of emerging life that one might suppose there was a producer, a director or a talented camera man's ever changing lenses to catch man in a film in which man does not necessarily subdue the giant turtle nor the hawk behave himself in the presence of the doves. Walt Whitman had become convinced that we ride forward on the shoulders of our ancestors. We look to the poets for hints of the future for prescience and for an answer to the tantalizing eternal question, "What is it?"

Business lawyers and business managers are not likely to volunteer an answer. The apes may seek an answer and the starling trill one. But can anyone of you find it when all the lights are extinguished and the sound is hushed? The wind blows with hurricane force. The sea rages, slapping the air. Then, man bends his knees and leans forward against the wind. His great cape blows out and for a moment or two it seems he will be carried aloft. He does not know what it is or whether it has a meaning. But, he is alive in a storm with trillions of creatures great and small, all drawing for a little air, a little nitrogen, a little fire-giving chemical and all are satisfied by the same planet, spinning in a somewhat haphazard arc, some 23.27 degrees off the vertical. It is possible to suppose that Gods who put him there, or even a single God, can maintain some interest in how man is faring along with the electric eel and amontillado, the ant-eater. Yet, this fearful lonely person, arms outstretched, standing on the clammy beach at nightfall is defying all other things, all the round things, the liquid things, the ghastly things, the heavy things, the light things, defying all these things as he asks for the Lord to favor him, to treat him specially, to bequeath on him all the benefits of the Universe but not any of its responsibilities. He is a giant in consumption of benefits but stingy in paying for them. He did not build the world, he only used it. That use was painful as well as profitable and surely he must not be responsible since he is only a sliver of light, a tap of the molecule, insignificant and alone. Surely, it is not right that he should pay for it.

Whether man's movement is that of a frozen sparrow caught in an ice slide on a hill or whether to some degree he controls his tomorrow, he is not still; not at rest; not a small muscle of the universe which atrophies in despair and uselessness. He is a grand creature who jumps upwards, his water apron falling in his flight; his arms are brawny, his fists are large. He demands to find some meaning in his existence, and by heavens, he will.

MALCOLM A. HOFFMANN
New York, New York
October, 1994

Early Childhood

Since truth is not rooted in time nor space and has a back as slippery as a water eel, one should not expect that young men or old men can hold on to it very firmly. Some of the material in my recollections was written more than half a century ago, some I have dictated today. Perhaps, if "catch the truth" is the game, it is just as important that these words span half a lifetime as it is that they span half a century. Certainly, they are purer, if not "truer" now since at my age there is no position to be gained through the use of the printed word. Yet I retain a positive ambition to put my life experiences together. Perhaps others will read them and be amused or saddened, but for me there is a meaning in just doing the exercise, in keeping my thoughts and intuitions alive. I have recorded many of the things I saw and how I understood them, using insight at hand and recollections sometimes contemporaneously recorded.

White Plains, New York, was my coddling, my burgeoning and my youth. I was born in Brooklyn, New York on November 26, 1912, at a point in time when there were only 47 states, horse-drawn trolleys were still to be found, and farmers far away used buckboards and horses to move around on freshly-loamed roads where one could always find the not unpleasant odor of horse dung. If you sat next to the driver you could smell the very tart smell of freshly oiled reins. It was a clean-air world, capable of carrying fragrance. I was three or four years old when first we lived in White Plains but able to venture forth through the open backdoor and screen door of our home during a period when the use of locks was not commonplace and burglaries almost unknown. I do remember some specifics from this early childhood period. Pots and pans were hung on hooks above the kitchen coal range. Soon the range was replaced, of course, by gas and electricity. Indeed, I remember that my house before 1918 had electric lighting fixtures which were constructed in combination with gas fixtures, the little gas jets emerging from the top and electric bulbs from the bottom of the fixtures. If the electricity failed, you could turn on the gas. This, of course, was one of the compromises with technology that people tended to make, tentatively, not sure of the new. Alexander Pope had said: "Be not the first to cast the old aside nor the first to embrace the new." I think that was the spirit of the early century. It was soon to be replaced by the notion that the newer is the better, would give us undreamed of happiness, and that technology was not to be resisted. And so with the refrigerator in our kitchen. An ice man came every morning wearing a rubber apron and with large forceps holding a square of ice of either 50 or 100 pounds. This was placed in the upper lefthand side of the icebox which, surprisingly, with its shelves and porcelain otherwise looked modern. During the day the machine worked very well, but before the ice man returned it was necessary to take the melted ice out of the big tray under the icebox, open the back door and throw the water on the grass. This became one of my chores in the early days. Children then often had "chores", quaint as this may sound today. Chores were not limited to the Amish nor even obsoleted by technology. Our furnace circulated hot air through vents opening into grids in each room. One of the chores each night was to damper the fire in the furnace. If this were not done correctly, smoke would seep through the vents, causing dire consequences such as smarting eyes, and in the imaginary fury of life — possible death by asphyxiation. My brother and I had the dampers correctly lined up at night.

As for the pots and pans, I remember well that I was about five years old, dressed in white, when a rumble of noise came up Chatterton Parkway to my house. It moved from house to house and got louder and louder as it neared my curious ears. The date was November 11, 1918, to be celebrated for many years as Armistice Day, later converted into Veterans Day. The war with the Germans and their allies was over, and the news climbed up the hill to be celebrated by children grabbing pots and pans and flowing out of their homes into the street making as much noise as they possibly could.

I grabbed a big pot and a small frying pan which I used to swing together in a crude clapping fashion. The noise was loud and good, but there was a little grease on the bottom of the frying pan, which ultimately was transferred to my white shirt, a matter which my mother noticed ere this great celebration was over.

Led by presidents of brotherly decent principles, this country for a time was consumed by a sense of egregious self-righteousness. We believed in democracy and said so, no matter what happened in the State Houses. The mood was exemplified by a totally obscure ditty which was very popular with children and yet made no sense whatsoever. It ran:

> "Eany, meany, miny, mo
> Catch a Tiger by its toe,
> if it hollers, make it say
> I surrender to the USA."

Somewhere in my very early years a more ancient ditty "catch a nigger by the toe" was used. Tiger was substituted over "nigger" about the time of the Armistice. Neither form seemed to make any sense, although it was possible that buried in the Old South was some reason for the ditty. Certainly it was better to use "tiger" than black people if they were to be caught by their toes. Perhaps, it was just as well to have tigers say, "I surrender to the USA". We would not want anarchistic tigers in our midst.

America! My father, who died when I was nine, had as a college student written a beautiful piece expressing his joy and gratitude for being a thinking citizen of this country. It was not considered naive or simple to make expressions of this sort. When I was in White Plains High School I won the "extemporaneous" (well prepared) speaking contest with remarks entitled "Thank God I am an American". There may have been some who thought this protestation of faith a little insipid, but they were not students in White Plains High School at that time.

We had everything going for us, including nature itself. I remember in this period that I ran down the street during a rain storm pausing to cup my hands to collect rain water and drink it from my palms for its freshness and purity. The grass was green in a way which I think no longer is found in this country. Now there is less green unmixed by dirt, weeds and discolorations of all sorts. Automobiles rode down our block at an average of about 5 passings per hour. Their arrival caused great excitement. The fronts of the cars in the 1920s were all different and there were many different makes since automobiles frequently had their engines made by a common source such as Lycoming Motors in Buffalo and their bodies crafted by local tinsmiths who called themselves automobile makers and to some extent mastered the assembly line using different molds of the tin, and very different name plates.

18 Longview Avenue in White Plains, our next residence, was on a flat, straight road that ran a mile or so from our house onto a small ridge. We often sat on the grass near the curb and played the game of identifying cars. The sharp-eyed, and I was one of them during this period, could see from afar a Marlin rolling down the hill or a Packard, a Reo, a White Swan, an Essex, Moon, a Graham Paige, a Studebaker, a Nash or a Pierce Arrow and there were many, many more, all with unique fronts.

The air was unpolluted, though the homes were heated by coal, but the furnaces burnt only in the winter. Kitchen coal stoves were warmed by a few embers of coal which were placed in the range by lifting the handle of an iron cover and an occasional replenishing application of coal from a bucket which was a standard apparatus in the kitchen in the early days of the century. The burning coal, however, was not sufficient to have any noticeable effect on the atmosphere. There weren't enough cars to do that and the country air was crisp and sometimes biting when it was cold.

The 1920s were for individual achievement. The public schools gave everyone the promise of a stake. The goal was not often to be a captain of industry or finance, but many school teachers, police, carpenters, plumbers and others from the hardworking professions and crafts had their aspirations realized by publicly financed schooling through the high school level. Many state universities had opened without tuition charges for residents and with nominal charges for out-of-staters. There was good enough distribution of wealth so that all might aspire to a house and later a car in White Plains; that legendary city with its 20,000, had an armory, a Main Street, and, of course, two movie houses which showed double features (2 full length movies) and often had vaudeville as well.

At the time of my birth the automobile had only just replaced the carriage, and I was spared television until fully grown. I had the distinction of being delivered by a Scottish obstetrician. According to my mother's report he declared me a fine Scotch bairn. My mother, during her confinement, was reading Sir Walter Scott's Lady of the Lake and with the encouragement of the obstetrician named me Malcolm Arthur. Since we Jews honor our ancestors by bearing their names it is believed that in some family bible Malcolm Arthur's deceased forbearer probably was written as "Moses Aaron." It is most unlikely that Malcolm and Arthur were included among my forbearers. As with other Jewish customs, dilution of name to fit the environment is commonplace and ancient names filtered down to first initials.

I don't remember Brooklyn or even Manhattan, where we lingered for a year to two after my birth, but by age three the family had moved to White Plains, New York. I stayed in that suburban paradise from babyhood until college age and my memories of it are fresh and vibrant even now, which is more than I can say about my stay in Chicago just two weeks ago.

I had a brother who was three years older than myself and a younger sister who died when I was six. My grandparents, except for my mother's father, were almost unknown to me. They both died at early ages. My father died when I was nine. Death and its loneliness were seemingly always my important companions.

I never learned Hebrew, although my grandfather was a Rabbi, but I learned phonetically the Kaddish prayer — the prayer for the dead. I did not know its meaning, but its cadences and swells beat strongly in my head and with the same sublimity as an oratorio by Handel, or a dark passage from Sibelius. It seemed to me that the impermanence of life was an ever-present fact. Death was not to be understood, nor even reckoned with, but it was some shadowy creature walking alongside who was prepared to tap me on the shoulder at any moment with an announcement of ominous significance. A poet, I believe he was Mark Van Doren, described death as a great white horse with a soft round nose.

At about age seven or eight, I saw a movie called "The Four Horsemen of the Apocalypse." The text had been written by Ibanez and perhaps it was a Cecil B. DeMille colossus. On a number of occasions the camera lifted to the sky where one was exposed to the four horsemen — Famine, Disease, War and Hatred. They all rode as skeletons on horses in the sky, carrying scythes and clubs, ready to beat down mankind. For months after seeing the movie as I sat on my front porch and looked up into the sky I could — if the clouds were right (grey and menacing) — see those four horsemen riding as they had in the movie. This was not an extraordinary experience for me because, when "The Ten Commandments" played at Loew's Strand I had once or twice seen among the cumulus clouds the great head of Moses with his long white beard, beaming down on me, and instructing me to follow the Ten Commandments, and avoid such false deities as Baal and the golden calf, whoever they were.

I remember the Loew's Strand because it also hosted vaudeville and once starred Balto, an Alaskan huskie, who with great courage pulled the sled carrying a potent serum from Nome to Fairbanks, quelling an epidemic. After the show, he and his master were stationed in the parking lot behind the movie house on Main Street. I petted this motheaten, unhappy dog and took his picture with my sixty-nine cent Kodak pin-hole Brownie camera. There was no glass in the camera, but it took good pictures if the light and wind were right.

We were impressionable people when the world and we were young and the green grass had moisture on it in the morning, and night walkers which could be captured at dusk and placed into a jar for fishing. We were not quite the free spirits of Mark Twain — neither Huckleberry Finn nor Tom Sawyer, but we were far nearer to them than to the tired-eyed youngsters who demand of indulgent or desperate parents that they be permitted to stay up through the late show. Fred Allen, the juggler, was at the Strand with a comic deadpan routine. There were always acrobats, musical saws, mono wheel cyclists, harmonica players and amazing exercises on the xylophone. These were all incident to the movies: the endless serials-part 73 of Reginald Denny in the *Leather Pushers*, Pearl White and Eddie Polo in *Do or Die*, and the chef d'oevure, the reason we parted with our quarters, the feature (and sometimes double) film. The double feature (romantic and Wild West) was the showcase for Norma Talmadge and Pola Negri (known as the "vamp" and, therefore, terrifying to little boys who were not aware of the difference between vamp and vampire). Bill Farnum (he shot from both hips simultaneously while on his horse's back) had other less skillful successors such as Tom Mix or William S. Hart and had many idolatrous young fans. My memory is disgorging these ancient heroes who are now unknown, just to preserve memory, mine or yours.

By 1925, the movies were supplemented by radio with its comics and sweet music. There were great voices telling us the news: Graham McNamee (who succumbed to sinful spirits while broadcasting the Rose Bowl game), David Ross, Milton Cross, Harry Hennesey, Kenneth Roberts, Bob Trout and others who are remembered not for what they said but how they said it.

As a small child I read of the American revolution. I gulped down details of the backwoods engagements in which the Deerslayer and other famous scouts created by James Fenimore Cooper and Joseph Altschuler followed the British and Indians to bloody engagements with the French on the Plains of Abraham, along the shores of Lake Erie and in the Hudson Valley. I read with my feet up high, my head sealed against the metal headboard of my brass bed made by Uncle Jack's company..

In my mind, the champion of the woods wore a deer skin cap, carried a large powder horn on a strap across his shoulder, and in his hand held a long musket, into which a plunger primed the powder. The place where the musket balls were carried was never made clear to me. The scout walked in soft moccasins, decorated in colored beads in an arc across the top front, moccasins purchased or taken from an Indian. His step was so silent that even the sharp ears of the Onondaga could not hear him ten paces away in the forest.

She was brave and generous, my sister, Gertrude, my great playmate one year younger than I. I think I remember her curls, and how beautiful her face was. I remember her standing gloriously erect and teasing me because of my sailor suit while she wore a nurse's uniform with a red cross on her breast, and my older brother a soldier's suit. Next, I remember that my brother and I were shunted out of our house and taken to an aunt's after we had a glimpse of our sister gasping for breath. "The paddle dips ... silence again." World War I's influenza had taken another victim.

Some twenty-five years later, my brother wore a soldier's suit, an infantryman's suit, in France, and Germany, and fought a grim war with live bullets.

In World War II, I spoke with my father's friend who had headed the Army Hospital at Fort Jay during World War I. He had been given no power to separate doctors from other draftees. Because of inflexibility of classification of recruits, the doctors often drilled with the infantrymen outside the hospital doors and inside poorly trained nurses were compelled to do doctors' work. This process of birth and death for the most part formed and turned by an almost endless series of accidents, does not seem to me to be controlled by reason, supernal or otherwise..

My father was about 6'3" tall, thin, Lincolnesque, and among his many achievements, a very capable lawyer. It is said that he spoke nine languages and when he was a law student early in the century, he served as an interpreter at the court and could generally handle any foreign language that came along. He would pick up a language because his ear was true and he was aware of the similarities in structure and etymological origin common to the different languages of the West. He came to this country from Moscow in the 1880s along with five sisters and brothers. Unlike most Russian Jews, the Hoffmanns had been blessed by the circumstances that they lived in Moscow as first-class citizens by courtesy of the Czar and had substantial resources. My great grandfather is said to have run a sizable Austrian factory manufacturing a well-known perfume, and was invited by the Czar's government to bring this industry to Moscow.

The next generation of the family left Russia for my grandfather to exploit a patent he held on an unbreakable doll. He traveled in style with a tutor for the older children, a governess for the babies, and he opened the American Doll and Toy Mfg. Co., with "absolutely unbreakable" dolls. The patent from the United States Patent Office bears the number 480,094 and is dated August 2, 1892, and it also carried a most descriptive title; "A composition for and Method of Making Heads and Limbs of Dolls."

It is said that a salesman for the doll company would bring a hammer along and demonstrate that the "White House" doll was unbreakable by smiting it with the hammer. It also has been said that my grandfather was the inventor of the "Teddy Bear", a doll made in honor of Teddy Roosevelt, and still cherished by the young, but it should be pointed out that many other companies made the same claim, and for all I know with as much or greater validity although I have found a contemporary record consistent with the Hoffmann claim.

The manifest of the steamship, D. Lahn, out of Newark, shows that on May 24, 1892, Frau Flora Hoffmann and Kinder Nebst Bedienung and Fraulein Helene Hoffmann and Fraulein Theresa Hoffmann all were traveling from Bremen to New York on a steam vessel. The vessel seems to have been equipped with four large smokestacks and four large masts and sails. The sails, and not the motor were auxiliary. The Hoffmanns had made an earlier landing and established a beach-head on these shores about six years before.

I have a photograph which shows my grandfather, a handsome bearded man with powerful shoulders and an aesthetic face. Legend has it that he was taller than my father and almost as tall as I. I reached 6'6" at the age of 18, but suddenly stopped growing. (I do, however, have three grand-sons now fully grown, two at 6'6" and one at 6'7".)

I remember vaguely my grandmother who seemed to me something of a roly-poly, but genial and exuding good spirits. When my grandfather died (in 1906), my father, as the oldest son, ran the doll factory for a while, and had to be the main support of his family. He was student, factory entrepreneur, lawyer and, for siblings, substitute father all in one. It is said that he rarely slept any length of time and never flagged in energy. Regrettably, and perhaps for this reason, my primary recollections of my father are clouded in uncertainty.

The second son, Isaac Newton Hoffmann, became a talented journalist and an expert in matters of finance. He was assistant financial editor of the New York Times, wrote for the Journal of Commerce, and died at the age of 34 or 35 of what was called the "Spanish Influenza", reportedly striking him because of the enormous hours hc worked in 1918 for the war bond drive in New York City. I remember hearing some of the excitement accompanying his interviewing of ministers of finance and other foreign dignitaries. Reporting scoops could still be achieved in those days by initiatives such as going out into the harbor on the pilot's boat.

The next brother, Jack or Jacob, received a graduate degree in chemistry from Columbia where he taught for a while and invented a light metal alloy which was particularly suited for the making of metal beds (we used them), and tubular dinette furniture. He settled his bed and metal company in Chicago, Illinois, loosening by distance his tight bond to the rest of the family. Over the years he only occasionally came to New York. I was always delighted to be with him and drink "Black Cows", a substance which 1 believe consisted of crushed blackberries and ice cream. As I reached my teens, we played chess by mail, and when he died of multiple sclerosis at the age of 54, I was given his chess set which I still use more than four decades later. Near the end of his life, Jack maneuvered in an electric cart and was close to helpless, but he never lost his good spirits nor his clear mind. It goes without saying that unlike their biblical namebearers, Abraham, Isaac and Jacob did not linger long on this planet.

My Aunt Rebecca, the youngest of the siblings, became the founder of a progressive school called the Hoffmann School for Individual Development, Inc. She founded the school in 1921 and until 1984 it still existed as a vital organ of the community. It was given some publicity by a reference in "Auntie Mame", and it was a school where the love of children became the basis for education. Associated with it from time to time were such forgotten dignitaries in education as Felix Adler and Helen Parkhurst.

But beyond all others, it will be remembered for the leadership, from 1945 until her death in 1980, of that extraordinary educator, Anna Hoffmann, my wife. But at this point in my chronicle, all of this is a diversion.

I am writing of my father. Not long after he had bought a house in White Plains in 1915 and built a law practice, he was stricken with tuberculosis, the dread disease of that period. For some reason, people did not like to acknowledge that they had tuberculosis in their families. It was thought to be endemic among poor immigrants who lived in crowded unhygienic conditions. There was no drug effective against it. There is one now, but not against all strains of this dread disease. The most accepted cure was to expose the lungs to fresh air in the Adirondack Mountains, and one of the experimental cures was to sleep on porches in subfreezing weather in the hopes of conquering tuberculosis by the infusion into the lungs of fresh, clean air. Thomas Mann in *Magic Mountain* describes this treatment as being administered in the Bavarian Alps. My father experienced it at Saranac Lake in the Adirondack Mountains and it was from here and out of this pain that many of his beautiful, romantic letters to my mother originated.

I hope I may be excused in exposing the delicate relationship between my parents, but the sentiments and words are emblematic of the early part of the century and applications of similar words and sentiments have shaped me and my siblings, my children and perhaps their children, and in the future, those images will affect their children's children. Sentimentality may not be genetical, but certainly it is cultural and I believe it is a bastion against the vulgar leveling off of the human experience into some predetermined amoral animism. Sentimentality and myths of the human spirit live for him who is not alone, but shares our past while he joins in each racing moment. The modern condemnation that something is "unreal" or the admonition "join the real world", houses the overbearing assumption that the speaker owns "truth" or "reality". Generally, this view of truth is found to be equated with the acquisition or conservation of money, power or conquest, and the unreal world is disassociated from these objectives. I hold with those who, even as we near the end of the turn of the century, say beauty is truth and truth is beauty, and that is all we need to know on earth.

My father was asked whether he could stand the cold and play a part in the outdoor experiment at Trudeau Sanatorium in Saranac Lake. He was told that he might freeze to death, but it was hoped that exposure, short of that, might cure the tuberculosis. Out of the star-full nights sleeping on Adirondack porches, came little lyrics and sentimental letters addressed to my mother whom he always referred to as "Dear Heart". I remember a small poem which he sent to my mother and which she often recited:

> There is only one star in the heavens
> As I look out of my window tonight,
> And you can see the same star from
> your window
> If you look, my true love, for its light.

There may have been other verses in which this small lyric was embedded, but I have no memory of them. On a Thursday night my father wrote to my mother:

> Dear Heart:
> It certainly is well that our story is one that "never gets old" else the ways of the mails would exasperate me. Just as I acknowledged your Sunday letter yesterday, I acknowledge your Monday letter today—and this is Thursday!

The author of the letter in 1919 was in Saranac Lake and the recipient of the letter resided in White Plains, New York, some 350 miles away. It would seem that mail was delivered far more quickly then than it is now, at least in this part of the country. I have read somewhere that the regular crosstown horsedrawn barouche in 1776 went from the East River to the Hudson River along 42 Street in 15 minutes. A Mercedes Benz cannot do it in that time today, except at 5 a.m. Dad's letter goes on, mentioning a friend who declined the porch treatment because he was afraid of being experimented with. Dad says:

When I found that the only "experiment" part was the bed treatment, I accepted eagerly — since I have become something of a believer in it myself. At any rate my first *three* weeks are up tonight. Let's both feel confident that I'll graduate in due course — a p.c. or "perfect cure" as they call it.

Mother apparently had complained that father's letters were not loving enough, and his letter goes on:

I know I don't put *enough* in. How could I? But "not a bit"? If you are still of that opinion I should be quite desperate for a means to convey an indication of my feelings.

Perhaps you can put your ear to your pillow and hear my old familiar heart beats. At the prescribed hours during the day I count them and they seem regular and orderly enough. But in the afternoon and at night — when in other words I'm in your arms — I don't count but I'm aware of a different sort of a beat! An imperative beat that won't be denied! And then I turn around and place my head in the nest — and the beats get fainter and fainter —

and a wonderful peace comes again! The same peace that I felt with my head in your lap the day before you left!

God bless you! Your Lover

He died at 39, when I was 9. He had spent 3 or 4 years from ages 29-33 as a tuberculosis patient in Trudeau Sanatorium. With this and other difficulty, he still dominated his family while he lived, in a curious and perhaps negative way. In all innocence, he had become an absent father. Our home on Longview Avenue made him a commuter, and he used the service of the New York Central Railroad which in those days had a 39 minute scheduled run from White Plains to New York City made with precision on trains that were clean and whose windows could readily be opened to let in the fragrance of woodlands that surrounded the railroad tracks for a long stretch. I am told that today the scheduled time is the same, but that the trains are rarely on time and that some of the same rolling stock that carried my father seventy years ago may still be found in use.

Dad often worked late in New York City on briefs or on other needs of litigation, calling at the last minute to say he would not be home. We children waited around wistfully hoping he would join us for dinner, when we were very young standing in the corridor behind the front door awaiting his brisk step. He was a worker incarnate, a Benjamin

Franklin hero, the proud inheritor of the Judeo-Puritan tradition of the necessity to work and succeed. Yet he was a gentle and soft-spoken man who could be as charming as any gentleman from Ireland.

The days were not long enough for him. He went through City College in the Class of 1901 taking substantial charge of the doll factory at the same time, acting sometimes as a translator in court for one or another of the nine languages which he had at his command. When his father died, my father was 22. He stood in loco parentis for two brothers and three sisters. He took a teacher's license on the basis of a competitive examination and briefly taught in our public schools while apparently sustaining his other pursuits. It was said that when he was not working, he was reading and when he was not reading he was smoking.

He played strong chess and taught all his children how to play, leaving behind an inheritance which enabled my brother to become an expert, and my brother's son an international master. My father used to say that chess was a snare. It was too easy for work and too hard for play. The meaning was not obscure. A good chess player or a "working" player must study chess as intensively as any other discipline. Its literature is large, its patterns can be mastered from books, i.e., from the study of the games of great players over the centuries. It is a tease for the mind, a substitute for despair and an all-consuming way of life if the player will let the game take command of his consciousness. I remember that my brother as a student cut out masters' games from the papers and kept them in his wallet playing them out in his head while he rode the subway or otherwise seemed to be inactive. Chess is warfare. It is also a gentle challenge of the mind. One can be defeated without loss of caste. He can prevail without diminishing his opponent. It is only among the professionals, the great players, that the stakes of victory are high — and that the game, like the game of tennis, has ceased to be a sport.

When I first learned tennis in my early teens there was a courtly etiquette that went with it. If your opponent said that your shot was out, even though you knew it was in by six inches, you accepted his judgment since he was closer to the ball. Sometimes if a call was made in your favor, and you knew the shot was out, you double faulted or netted on the next play in order to equalize via sportsmanship the unfairness of the forces of nature. There was much calling out of questions like "Are you sure you're ready?", "Did I serve too soon?", inquiries which placed the player squarely within the gentilities described by Tom Brown at Rugby. It was only later that gamesmanship was discovered. Surely everybody remembers that auspicious moment when Stephen Potter, a middle aged Oxford don, was playing with a student whose mighty serves whizzed by and whose volleying seemed overwhelming. Only the resourcefulness of the don enabled him to prevail. Suddenly he clutched at his side and the student asked with concern, "Is there anything wrong, sir?" "Nothing, son, just my ticker." At this moment not only was gamesmanship borne, but tennis became a vicious, manipulative game. The corrosion of tennis was completed not on the Oxford Courts, but in the emergence of high stakes for the tennis player. Sportsmanship began to dwindle away, when $75,000 might ride on whether a shot was in or out. In chess, as the game became more organized spawning international competitions and invitations dependent upon numbered rank among the players, the tournament players began to lose enjoyment of the game in return for stakes piteously small compared with tennis, but often much more needed by the players. Perhaps even chess has been corrupted by the prize system. Not that a better system is available, but greed seems to be the foundation for most relationships among people, and has changed the character of sports.

I am not a cynic. I believe that certain people are better endowed with strength of muscles, strength of mind, strength of conscience than are others. Certainly these different talents may claim differing rewards from society. It is pretty much the same among the grizzly bear. But in our desires to create a better world through our own conduct, I think, we are still to be preferred to the koala bear.

I am positive that there is no animal other than man prowling the earth which concerns itself with right or wrong, good or evil, compassion, tenderness and decent social relationships. We may kill more effectively than other animals, but I also believe that we love more intensively. This is a great bundle of neurons and ganglions that we carry around in a vulnerable container of skin and bones. It kills at wholesale, but it also writes books about the misty future utopia in which persons will serve the high values of the community, creativity will flourish, and cruelty become unknown. And even the futurists have trouble keeping the human race intact for these utopias. My friend, Bob Jastrow, has already passed civilization's torch onto the computer and depicts a future in which hard-shell silicon intelligences will replace us. Professor Maisky of MIT said somewhere that we will be lucky if the computers permit us to stay on as pets in a human zoo.

Back to chess. I enjoyed the game but never truly studied it. I played well at my level of chess but far below that of my brother and nephew. I was not seduced by chess, but I was by other romantic games such as the necessity to lead a life in which "good" was a constant value, and human conduct was always to be appraised on some judgmental scale in which the highest level was the person who did the most for others, who lived up to Maimondies' level of charity — one who helps others without their knowing that they are being helped. My home was fiercely devoted to such values. I learned them from my mother who learned them from her father, who as a young rabbi, left his congregation in Leipzig, Germany, in order to fulfill a written contract obtained by correspondence with some Jewish families in Zanesville, Ohio. It is said that there were so few Jews in that community grandfather conducted his services on the front porch of the house afforded him by the congregation and kept the Torah in an improvised arc in the room known as his "parlor", now called a "living room". It was in his house that my mother was born. And it was there, I take it, that good and evil and right and wrong became a constant measuring stone in the quiet recesses of internal family debate. No one speaks aloud of such matters anymore, but deep in the untrained, almost subliminal, consciousness of a human animal are these ethical questions. Even now, I suppose their answers provide the principal hope for humankind's survival on this planet.

I hold in my hand some of the little records of life. Father received his degree of A.B. from the College of the City of New York in June of 1902, and received a professional certificate from the Department of Public Instruction from the State of New York which enabled him to teach in any public school of the State, dated August 1902. With this comes a whiff of memory. It was said that Dad taught in a high school of a neighborhood in New York that was much populated by Italian immigrants. A window at the first floor of the school house was kept open in the hot weather of these pre-airconditioning days. For reasons I cannot recall, a large student wearing a red bandana around his throat brandished a knife in a menacing manner in the direction of a fellow classmate. My father is said to have run from the front of the room in the direction of the young delinquent who, in turn, seeing that the chase was on, jumped through the opened window, with my father in close pursuit. Some blocks away, having gained only slightly on his long-legged teacher, the student sought refuge behind his father's fruit stand. The lad's father called out in protective Italian and put his cart and himself between his son and my father. My father then explained the mischief in Italian and the student's father discovered the knife in the clothes of the large muscular lad of about 15 or 16 years. The son offered no resistance, as his father drew him across his knee and then spanked him to the delight of numerous onlookers. The man instructed his son with many imprecations that in this new land which he was fortunate to share with others, he was an American who must respect his teacher and worship his schoolhouse. I can remember the story being told in just this way by my mother when America was still young and when learning was the priceless gift of

opportunity to countless immigrants, and teachers were respected as votaries at learning's altar.

When he moved on from teaching, Dad and his
good friend, Felix Frankfurter, registered at the
New York Law School. The New York Law School
had been set up just a year or two before as a result
of a schism created in the Columbia Law School
faculty over the case book method. That method
was the brain-child of Professor, later Dean,
Langdell of the Harvard Law School. The case book
method, as its name implies, brought the student
historically through emerging legal doctrine by
reading one case after another carefully to follow
the flow and change of legal thought in different
subject matters. This was a rather indirect and
difficult way of mastering law since the student
with the aid of his professor was required to pull
out the substance of law through an analytical
process. The more traditional method, and that
followed by New York Law School and Columbia
before the change, was to read commentaries, the
work of scholars who deduced the principles from
the cases and assembled them for reading digested
in book form. These two methods are still in use
and sometimes combined at different law schools.
According to Harold Phillips, Frankfurter, near the
end of his life, said he had studied at both New York
University and New York Law School before going
to Harvard and did not like either of them. Frankfurter, with his savings from a city inspector job

and family help, went to Harvard Law School. In his letters he urged my father to do the same. My father went through the courses at New York Law School and was admitted to the Bar of New York State on February 13, 1906. Curiously, the executed form evidencing his admission to the Bar shows "18...". This date is slashed through with a pen and "1906" written in its place. The courts then apparently were no squanderers of the people's money. At 22 years old he became a member of the Bar in this great new land which he loved beyond measure. By 1909 he had been admitted to the District Court of the Southern District and to the Circuit Court of the Second Circuit.

On November 26, 1912, according to a register which he kept and I have inherited, my father tried a libel case and won a fee of $75. It is likely that on the same day he was present when I was born, the latter proceedings handled in the evening by an obstetrician named Dr. E. K. Tanner. The register shows that Tanner was also a client of my dad, which is as it should be, since this amiable Scot was responsible for my being named after a great Scotch hero.

One ducks for apples in selecting memories about mother. She died almost 50 years ago, but sometimes I can still hear her tender, soft, voice commanding in its elegance of expression. I knew her mostly as a widow stripped of her modest inheritance by the depression and it seems to me that her tone of voice later acquired a fiber of helplessness. When the depression grabbed the land in its uneven, spasmatic hold, it seems to me that it squeezed hardest those who had some property but not the skill to hold to it. My mother had invested in White Plains real estate the insurance left behind when father died, making wrong choices for the right reasons. For example, she bought a piece of commercial property on the Post Road rather than on Mamaroneck Avenue, reasoning that an artery which ran from White Plains to New York City would be more likely to develop than one which crossed Westchester from White Plains to the Sound. Within a decade, Mamaroneck Avenue burgeoned into the great shopping center of White Plains, while Post Road showed little improvement. A movie theatre dickered for a few minutes about the purchase of my mother's property on the Post Road, but the depression was already deep and after an exciting solicitation the theatre company decided against the purchase. The bank eventually took the home in which we had lived for 15 years. The bank also took her two-family house to which we had briefly moved after the loss of our original home. My mother bravely held the family together from 1922 for about a decade—long enough for us to get well established in college, but then disaster came. The little real estate business she established was utterly nonproductive and she had no place to turn except inward. This delicate and sensitive woman developed what was then called involutionary melancholia, but which today would simply be called depression. She held on to her dignity and self-poise long enough to see me graduated from Harvard College in 1934. Thereafter, her decline was quick and her inner forces were no longer able to withstand the assaults of fear and uncertainty.

I tend to think of her at an earlier time explaining to me how, as a girl in Brooklyn before the turn of the century, she had studied art in a Catholic school. Dominating our living room was a full-sized painting of Evangeline running in a meadow of flowers beset with vivid green grass and carrying a colorful garland of long white daisies. I can see the painting now very well with my eyes closed and, as a boy, I thought it very fine. Perhaps it was a copy of a museum painting since art students of that era often trained by copying in museums. My mother's sister, Saide, had attended the same convent. Dominating the living room in her Brooklyn apartment was a picture of a blind Milton dictating to his daughters. With his dour face, the dark colors, the whole picture seemed to exude both the terror of darkness, and the heroic triumph of man over his environment. Overall, the painting made the room so gloomy that I did not want to play there. This one was definitely a museum copy.

When we were young we were surrounded by sets of books. It was the tradition to buy the full works. The Marie Antoinette Edition of Alexander Dumas's works was some 30 volumes. I read most of them in delicious hours after school with a sense of being a gallant swordsman. My sword always stood at the service of her majesty, ready to battle alongside Athos, Porthos and Aramis. Dickens was present in some 20 volumes; Mark Twain, perhaps 10. And everywhere there were English author sets. My first series was *Journeys through Bookland.* Another set was called *French Classical Romances* and there also stands out in my mind, a gift of an aunt on my eleventh birthday, a collection of some 35 volumes of Sir Walter Scott under the title the *Waverly Novels*, each printed on very thin onion skin paper and in a small size that could be held in the hand. These beautiful little books could be read behind a tree, stuffed into a pocket, and went well with graham crackers and milk. "Kenilworth" was exciting, but "Ivanhoe" was the most read, most discussed at the time I was 10 or 12 years old. It was hard to understand the fuss made about the Knight Templar being in love with a Jewish girl. But it was this story which perhaps for the first time introduced me to anti-Semitism as found in the literature of England and which has remained alive throughout my lifetime.

I remember little red-headed Frankie Bell, a splendid athlete who later on captained our high school football team, and who served as my inseparable companion at the age of 8 or 9. There came, however, the day when he invited me to attend Sunday services with him at the Congregational Church in White Plains. In some confusion I said I would have to ask my mother. She seemed astonished at the suggestion but said to me you may do so, but only if you tell Frankie you are Jewish and invite him to join you for service Saturday at the Synagogue. I dutifully did as my mother had said and my friendship with Frankie Bell came to a sudden end. I was bewildered when he would no longer talk to me in the schoolhouse. It was not until much later on when, as a college student, I began to hear about Hitler's atrocities against the Jews that I became attuned to the existence of anti-Semitism as an aspect of life in this country as it is in Germany, France, England and elsewhere.

At Harvard in 1930 no Jewish students would dare to tread in the doors of some of the social clubs and even the comic magazine building, the Lampoon. A great Harvard alumnus, Arnold Hoffman (no kin to me), told me the following: He and his two brothers were raised in Roxbury, Massachusetts, and in order to attend the Boston Latin School, had to come through a tough neighborhood where Jews were despised. Although he was not a big man, he was quite muscular and developed a system that made him the lead-off man in a wedge of three brothers who would never get off the sidewalk when confronted by a hostile gang. They did land blows on the enemy, however, with great positiveness and speed. Hoffman developed such skill in battling his way to school that by the time he reached college age he had become a semi-pro boxer helping to support his brothers with their Harvard tuitions. These brothers later handsomely endowed Harvard and I am told gave a scholarship to which only "C" men were eligible, thinking this group the most neglected by the authorities.

This Hoffman boy went out for the football team in the period just before World War I, in or about 1917. As he crossed the threshold of the locker room, a large New England Brahman type opposed him and said, "We have no Jews on the Harvard football team." As Hoffman told me the story a half century later, he was on his way to the Boston Latin school once more where the quickness and power of his fists counted and he decked this 6'3" lineman with one quick blow to his jaw. He had no trouble thereafter and made the team. I was told by the receptionist in my law office that although she was either the first or second best tennis player in her university in Florida, the tennis coach blocked her from the team because he didn't want a Jewish name on the program as representing the university.

"Frisky" Merriman, a history professor at Harvard, swung a pointer back and forth over a blackboard marked with "freedom" on one end and "tyranny" on the other end, saying that history was like a metronome leading inexorably from freedom to tyranny and back again but with no discernible forward direction towards a better world; I never believed this, but I now accept that he may have been right as we celebrate a great military victory in Iraq although no one still knows why young men must die, or why we fought, or whether we achieved our objectives in this victory. And now, more than a year later, there is lamentable acknowledgment that we were misled about the extent of our victory.

My consciousness of being a Jew was sharpened and made poignant by the German experience of my European co-religionists, but, starting at an early age, I did not take kindly to religion. I tended to think of God as a benevolent figure in the sky and when He lost His benevolence, I lost Him altogether.

My mother's father, Marcus B. Newmark was a Rabbi. In 1879 he had settled in Zanesville, Ohio, where my mother was born. Zanesville was generally famous for having experienced, along with Johnstown, a great flood in the 1880s when my mother was a little girl. The flood generally called the "Johnstown Flood", always was called the "Zanesville Flood" by my mother in her racontage. Newmark came to Zanesville because by correspondence with the Jewish community of that little city, he had contracted to come to head a Synagogue not knowing that the members of his congregation would be no more than a few handsful. Newmark had served a Synagogue in Leipzig where, in accordance with family legend, Newmark fathers and sons had served for many generations as Rabbis. After a half-dozen years he moved from Zanesville to Elmira, New York and then to Albany, next, to Harrisburg, Pa., and finally - resettled in Brooklyn where he headed a large congregation.

When I was 12 years old, I was informed that I needed to be instructed for Bar Mitzvah, that splendid ceremony from which a boy is supposed to emerge a man in the religious community. To accomplish this end, it was necessary that I learn some prayers in Hebrew and also that I make a speech in English. My grandfather, however, insisted that I must receive my training in his home in Brooklyn, and so a schedule of 15 or 20 visits was arranged in the course of which I was to receive instruction in the Hebrew language and master my prayers. Travelling some 35 miles from White Plains to Brooklyn was a big logistical undertaking even for a 12 year old who was close to 6' tall. The result was that I arrived on the Brooklyn scene only 3 or 4 times and soon it became apparent that I could not be taught Hebrew under these circumstances. Consequently, my grandfather wrote out the Hebrew prayers in English phonetics, an heroic undertaking since the prayers were lengthy, and as I tell it, he also wrote my speech, an important part of the ceremony. I hope I do not depreciate him by my recollection that the ghost speech started, "I thank my grandfather without whose aid this ceremony would not have taken place."

Mamaroneck Avenue Junior High School

In 1925, Mamaroneck Avenue Junior High School was located on Mamaroneck Road in White Plains; it was a separate educational stop on the way to high school, college, and finally professional schools. Our eyes, and our ears were open to learning at 12 or 13, and some of us had even been taught to listen.

Not only did Mr. Jacobs give us the Argonauts and the rudiments of Latin, but we had courses in general science, and geography, the last being something more than a listing of the States and their capitals. It showed us a little of the dynamism in the country's growth and the need to find ways to bring the produce of the great plains to seaports. Of course, we also had mathematics, which went up to plain geometry, but we did not have the quick moving mathematical analysis of today which throws trigonometry at the student at an early age.

Trig was not available until the last years of high school and in between there was solid geometry, enough to make those who felt unsuited for mathematics know that they are cretins.

There were some clubs, and the rudiments of self-government, all preliminary to the great political and learning explosion which took place during the three-year session at White Plains High School.

On a shadowy path before junior high were the "grades" taking us from ages 6-12, I have some difficulty 70 years later in charting this progress, but I'll try.

On return from grade school at the end of the school day, I often was met at least halfway by my glorious collie named Bruce. "Scots, wha hae wi' Wallace bled, Scots, wham Bruce has aften led, Welcome to your gory bed, Or to victory!" Bruce was a blue merle collie which I bought out of my allowance and life's savings and twenty weeks of future allowance which were advanced to me by an affectionate mother. Bruce was killed, along with several other neighborhood dogs, by a neighbor woman, who placed arsenic in pieces of beef which she placed around her lawn. This atrocity was not discovered, however, until after Bruce had died with some paroxysm and foaming in his mouth which resulted in Dr. Fabricus, a most careful physician, giving our family the rabies treatment. It didn't seem to matter that none of us was bitten. It was "better to be safe than sorry" was one of the slogans of the time, and he followed it, injecting a heavy, wide-diametered needle (German, circa. 1900) into our bellies — all three bellies: my mother, my brother and myself, every afternoon for twenty-seven days. Within a few days our dogs had been exhumed and sent to the Rockefeller Institute, where it was learned that they did not have rabies but had died of the arsenic poisoning. I do not remember that anything was done to the "poor old lady" who lived down the block, but readily would have put arsenic in her soup had I been given the chance.

Now we had started the study of Latin, Bob Baum and I instituted a club called "Nobilus Amicus", not truly recognizing that the reference was to a single noble friend, rather than many. We seemed, ourselves, to be the only full time members of this sapient group, but even that would have required the plural.

One day the two of us were walking away from the school house and delighting in tales about our Latin teacher who, I seem to remember, had the wonderful quality of being overweight and equipped with duck feet. We had made certain unpleasant remarks about him until, hearing footsteps, I turned around and discovered that Mr. Jacobs, the Latin teacher, was walking directly behind us no more than a few feet away. It is probably too apt for me to say I learned the lesson that in talking about people behind their backs I should be sure that they were not behind my back.

We played baseball and even football in junior high, but there were no tennis courts nearby and I was not to become a devotee of that game until several years later when public courts became available to me. We ran a good deal and talked a good deal. Sometimes, at ages 8 or 9, we collected nightwalkers on the lawn and as dusk came in, put them in mason jars with holes in the cap, added dirt, and saved them for fishing with our big brothers, a delight taking place only occasionally. The big brothers who permitted us to fish with them guided us to a quarry in North White Plains where it was said that the clear water was 300' deep. They had their reels, rods and spinning lines. Little brothers' fishing rods, on the other hand, were characterized by maple shoot poles with fixed strings attached to the ends and to iron hooks. Generally, hooks were put on the string by first accidentally attaching them to the thumb, leaving only a slight wound from extractions. Occasionally we caught some sunfish and once in a while a pickerel so small it had to be thrown back. But, mostly, — nothing but lost worms and a sunburn.

At school, our desk tops opened vertically. At age 8, I came in early on Valentine's Day and placed a store bought Valentine (a great prize) under the top of the desk belonging to the light of my life, Isabelle Mead. This was an act of love causing me to blush. My card was anonymous, for without any signal of favor from her I would not let Isabelle know I was her hidden admirer. I left the room and returned shortly after to find a rather crude Valentine in my desk, also anonymous. At the next desk there sat a scrawny girl whom it seemed to me was very disagreeable, but nonetheless had a love light for me in her eyes. It never occurred to me that anyone else might have put the Valentine in my desk. At the proper moment of changing study rooms and quite aware that I was being observed, I dropped this Valentine into a waste basket. This was an act of cruelty, but at the same time perhaps justified in putting off forever my most undesirable neighbor who was eight or eight and one-half years old. A day or two later I learned to my utter consternation from a classmate who was a keen observer of all the proceedings, that Isabelle Mead had put the Valentine in my desk and that the innocent girl at the next desk had nothing whatsoever to do with it. It took time to get rid of that torment, to get rid of that guilt and frustration; and to understand that I was not the love-light in my neighbor's eye.

Valentines Day had warm significance for me thereafter. When I was literate enough to do it, I began to rhyme Valentine with wine, fine, dine, supine, divine and contrived to make separate Valentines first to my mother and then a little later to a few glorious young ladies who for different weeks or months occupied my capacious heart. Thereafter, I wrote Valentine verses to my wife who received one every year from the year I met her until the year she died, a span of 46 years. She lay on a hospital bed, dying of cancer as she received my last Valentine doggerel containing these lines, written in red ink on paper with hand drawn hearts and arrows:

> Darling - this is St. Valentine's
> Day,
> And not the last - I'm glad
> To say.
> Darling - Will you, as you face
> this trial
> Hold my hand a little while?
> As you and I for many
> years
> Have conquered all our little
> fears.
> Let's us now for the forty-sixth
> time
> Face this day - one day at
> a time
> And for the greatest girl
> on all the line,
> Thank God, you are my
> Valentine.

My daughters were also recipients of these little tributes of love and they became very skillful at Valentine writing in their own rights. How much trouble these caused us over the years I do not know.

One afternoon a classmate and I walked by the house of the then most flirtatious soubrette in our class. She was sitting on the lawn with four or five other girl classmates when suddenly they waived us to come join them. I remember the scene only too well, the water sprinkler was cooling the lawn on a hot June day and as we approached this young lady suddenly lifted her skirt displaying the circumstance that she was not wearing panties, a sight which had devastating effects. Bob Baum and I began to run. We raced across the street and down the road and did not stop running until we arrived safely home - fire and brimstone. Whenever we saw that ambitious girl again, we averted our eyes and surrounded her with an air of sinfulness. We were not of an age to be seduced.

We stood erect and powerful in the 7th, 8th and 9th grades which composed our Junior High education. There was a sense of passage to the important state of almost teenagery as we left the 6th grade and began to study such imponderables as first year Latin and Elementary Algebra. Junior High School played no part in interscholastic sports. It was a time for growing bigger and in my town there were no gangs or menacing forces which necessitated street knowledge. There was plenty of time to dream of heroism.

Once in the eighth grade when I was already close to 6 feet tall, and 12 years old, someone called me a nasty name. I stood up to my full height and said, "Hit me first", a most menacing remark. This young man, however, accepted the invitation and I went home with a bloody nose to hear some dubious comments from my mother about when I should waive my peace loving qualities. She lived in a world of gentle knights and beautiful flowers. She painted and loved art, but was oppressed within a few years after 1922 when my father died by the necessity to live in a world of dollars and cents, which she never could fully understand.

Some values did emerge during this period. They were more or less absolutes because of our reading and idealizations rather than sensibly limited by hot and cold, love and desire. Even heroes remained outsized , not to be cut down by the media. For example, I did not learn that Babe Ruth was something of a drunk and disorderly character until many years after he died. Obviously, to most of us Babe Ruth was a god who on one occasion when the Yankees were playing Cleveland, pointed to the right field stands and to the total amazement of the fastball pitcher pushed a home run in the exact direction indicated. I didn't see the occurrence, but in one of the three games I attended in Yankee Stadium as a boy, the Babe did hit a home run. These were our heroes. William Tilden, the world's best tennis player, a man of dubious morality, was prosecuted on a morals charge. We knew only that he was an incomparable player who climbed heights of tennis stardom that made him the most famous player in the history of that sport. In other words, our heroes were super heroes although their character performances necessarily fell short of what we thought was the mark. The papers confined themselves to the players. The reporters were reporting baseball and not lechery.

They never referred to Babe Ruth as "the drunk" or William Tilden as "the homosexual". This shift in emphasis took more than half a century. My recollection is that the sports page never referred to the criminal activities or even the speeding tickets of the great sport stars. If they were men of low character the sports writer did not find it necessary to inform us, unless, indeed, the character failing had to do with changing the natural forces at play in the competitive game. There was much horror because the 1922 Chicago White Soxs (soon dubbed "the Black Soxs") threw a World Series game. "Say it isn't so, Joe" was the plaintive cry of a Chicago news boy as the mighty Joe Jackson, a consistent 400 hitter, walked by. Short of such a dark disaster, we did not know who stole from whom and indeed thought that sports were perhaps the purest forms of human activity.

At the age of 16, as a high school newspaper editor, I achieved a part-time job as a sportswriter for the newly opened White Plains Daily Press. I was given assignments by the Editor and paid for my work by the inch of lineal type. My recollection is that it came out to $2.75 a column of newsprint.

By hard work and lots of reporting that summer I achieved on one or two occasions about $30 a week, much to my own astonishment as well as to my mother's. But at the age of 16 I was asked to report on a prize fight at the local armory where an overweight welterweight champion in some obscure group such as the "Central Westchester National Guard" fought his challenger, a young man whose body seemed to contain some firm muscle structure. The champion, about 40 years of age, looked like a soft mail sack, but I was only a young sportswriter and did not know his history. In the second round of this fight in which no one seemed to be getting hurt, the champion threw a wild blow. I was sitting at ringside and to my astonishment, although the blow seemed to miss the head of the challenger by a foot, the challenger fell down, apparently knocked out. I reported what I saw to my paper and was rewarded by never being assigned to a prize fight again. I remember that the words suggesting impropriety in my report were removed from the story, which in the shortest possible number of words reported merely that the challenger was knocked out in the second round.

* * * *

Some of my earliest recollections of nature give prominence to trees — the tall oaks along the street where I was raised, shade trees offering escape from the burning sun. When young I sometimes invested trees with the pathetic fallacy that their sighing in the wind was a commanding sound which superseded all physical explanations for the noise. I have often told stories to little children — my own and others — of imaginary tiny elves who live in the trunks of the great tulip trees. Uniformly in my stories they were kindly spirits who emerged from their homes to wipe away tears or to enforce laughter by fiat. Consequently, I was not amazed to learn from Frazer's book, *The Golden Bough*, that among many peoples, trees are embodiments of the life spirit, that sacred groves were common among the ancient Germans and that old German laws placed ferocious penalties on whomsoever dared to peel the bark of a standing tree. Frazer tells us, "The culprits' navel was to be cut out and nailed to the part of the tree which he had peeled, and he was to be driven round and round the tree till all —-his guts were wound around its trunk."

The house where I spent my early boyhood was dominated by oak trees. These trees had a special significance in antiquity. It seems that the gods, including Jupiter himself, more often occupied the oak tree than any other. It also seems, according to Frazer, and I have no reason to disagree, that the oak tree is struck by lightning more often than any other. Apparently, with the logic man sometimes uses as a substitute for knowledge, it was decided early that the oak was sacred because the thunderbolt represented the passage of the great sky god whose awful voice is heard in the thunder as he descends from the sky to the tree. So lingering is this belief that even today, Christians use the mistletoe, a parasite which only grows on an oak tree, as part of their genial rites at Christmas time. Such explanations seem plausible to me because I am a lawyer who deals with obscure problems of law in which courts make associations as a result of the predilections of lawyers often more strange and less revealing than these old signs of the woods.

In my college days, I wrote a short story having to do with the death of my Father, and in it were sighing trees. In that story I described the bedroom of our house shared by my brother and me on Longview Avenue in White Plains and the sleepless nights we spent waiting for my Father to die. I remember now, that as a student at Harvard I submitted the story to Bernard DeVoto to satisfy a writing assignment. He liked the story but wrote on the margin the comment, "Why must everyone write about when they were children?"

One reason why the important experiences of childhood are registered sharply in memory is that young memory cells are not encrusted with the deceptions of experience. It is also true that first experiences are absolute and fresh. This is true of pain as well as pleasure. It is true of neutral objects: the uses and smell of a pencil, its softness to the bite, the pattern and the flatness and cleanliness of a fresh tablecloth. Even in these neutral experiences, objects inanimate build full and realizable meanings. A pencil to me today has no shape nor size nor color — it is merely a sharp or dull point. The tablecloth today is something rarely to be noticed except when pointed out by women. Things have lost full meaning and the universe of things has tightened into things basic, their functions register as good or bad for me, but the things now carry less uniqueness of their own.

This does not mean complete disappearance of the child beneath, the child who knows things immanently, tactically, in his heart and stomach, as well as in his mind. A child captures all the sensory meanings of things and some place deep in memory they are still there. The child stays within the aging frame as a prayer, nonetheless, until the state of adulthood specifies that he be expelled.

That night in my story my brother and I kept vigil until it was brought home to us that our Father had died.

I think we had thrown down a challenge to the Lord. We would accept him if Father lived, reject him if Father died. Perhaps the story I wrote at 19 years of age was only a story dramatizing and making great what was the bitter hurt with which I recalled my Father's death nine years before. My brother David did not remember this challenge. But without the manuscript before me I remember well the description of the tall trees swaying in the April wind, stretching outside our window, and the eerie shapes which the shadows of the trees made against the walls of our house and our garage. The trees swayed, clenched, and frightened me; the shadows, indeed, seemed the fingers of God. In my story, the challenge was a direct challenge to God himself, such as the one Eugene O'Neill's protagonist in THE DYNAMO hurled against the Lord; holding his fists above his head, he said in the bite of the thunderstorm, "Strike me dead now Lord." God failed to notice the challenge in DYNAMO. Ours certainly was worded differently. We threatened God that if my Father did not survive we would know there was no God. After Father died (I was 9, my brother 12) we began to lose the foundations of our religious beliefs. It may be urged solidly that a nine-year-old child should not have to challenge the Great Being of whom it is said that His ways passeth all understanding. For us God had been something real and immediate, something as tangible and apparent as our sleds, our lunch baskets and the path we followed to school. When God lost that quality, he did not disappear, but he lost his real meaning for us.

I knew very well what I was doing. I know my brother grew strong, but for me it took the better part of my life, backing and filling, going forward in faltering steps, returning again, gaining only a slow advantage in the encounter with the basic fears and loneliness of life. In recent years I have enjoyed within me the real content of having conquered fear in its more obvious forms, of having filled my life with love rather than with bitterness or hate. Please do not ask me to share this accomplishment of mine, won so painfully and laboriously, with God. This victory is mine. I remember having read somewhere the story of an English aviator downed over the North Sea early in the War. His plane came down in flames and he, badly burned, fell into the sea, maintained only by a Mae West. What sustained him in his pain and agony during lonely hours in the water before rescue was the realization that he was a man of strength, and that, unlike so many men of whom he had read, it was not necessary for him in his hour of extremity to turn to God, in whom he had not placed his belief during his lifetime.

People in the days of Epicurus, Aurelius, and Epictetus, seemed to have valued men by the way they died. The British aviator fell from the skies, flesh burning, living his last moment true to his own belief. I place this episode 1,000 cubits above any last minute confession or conversion or affirmation of belief subscribed to by sweating men frozen in panic, all of the ministers of the world to the contrary notwithstanding. Do not think of me, if you will, as an atheist because of these declarations. I am not. But at age 81, I think I am far too much of a man to believe that if a God exists the individuals' suffering, prayers and affirmations are things he is tuned into like a listener dialing different radio receivers. I think that if God exists it is sacrilegious to attribute to him the literary effort of the Bible. I think that if God exists, it also degrades him to assume that he is party to man's conflicts and his desires.

I am often impressed by the beautiful uniformity of nature as explained to me by my scientific friends. I am often impressed by the feeling that my life plays a part in an historically emerging process. I believe that others have lived before me, that others will come after, and somehow those who follow are better for their predecessors' efforts. In Whitman's words, we ride on the shoulders of our fathers. I cannot accept God as a chess player moving lives about on a board of 64 squares. I have little patience with those minds which have devoted their lives to justifying God to man. This I suppose is the most arrogant of the forms of human endeavor.

There is not a second-rate mathematician who does not think more clearly than Aquinas because logical thought does not rise above the premise with which it works. Christians who discuss the niceties of the Trinity cannot demonstrate that, 2,000 years after the birth of Christ a Christian treats his fellowman any better than he did before. Where then did all this theological effort lead? Was it only to give comfort to man dying or killing his fellowman? Perhaps it has given comfort to hopeless men by helping them to endure pain which might otherwise have been unendurable. Perhaps it has enabled some to die without tears. I suggest that such limited beatitudes are available without the interposition of organized religion. Because courage and will are self-developable muscles, it may be that religion has done man the disservice of weakening his soul. I think religion is nothing more than an expression of the smallness of man: "bow the head and bend the knee, and magnify the Holy One Praised be He,". I make no quarrel with humility. I prefer to look at the multitude of bright stars which beat out a code for a mysterious and infinite universe and wait for my fellowman to decipher it.

The Orange and the Black

(1927–1930)

I hold in my hand the 1929 "Oracle", the Year Book of the White Plains High School Graduating Class; a year book one year ahead of my class; why I possess it I do not know; I have also the "Oracle" for my graduating year, 1930. I am found in many pictures in these commemorative books, tall, skinny; near the back center of the photograph so that my height will not blank out the others. Many curious pictures of a tall, young man, high school Junior, and Senior, whose acquaintance to me by now is only a nodding, certainly not a friendly one. I think he wishes me well but feels a bit sorry for me, near the end of the road he is just about to walk. He stands back center in the picture showing contestants in the extemporaneous speaking contest, a contest which he won and in which he talked about books, peace and other things of the spirit which remain important to him, and represent mystiques, but not problem solutions. His face is full of hope.

The team lost the Roosevelt debate, again back center, with Roosevelt High School of Yonkers, but Yonkers came to the auditorium well prepared, and we thought we could glide by with eloquence and White Plains charm. Here is the Amphyctrons, the Honor Society, with the classic name. I am right up in front center. Next to that is the "Orange", the school newspaper. The "Orange" took much of my time for I was its Editor-in-Chief and I took my work seriously. I am standing next to my predecessor, David Clark, a step below him but our heads are at equal height, since I was about 6'5", and had not stopped growing. Justice Felix Frankfurter liked to be photographed on the first run of train steps while his tall wife, Margaret Denman, stood on the platform below.

The next page shows my picture in the Latin Club standing next to Alvah Tobias Otis, the teacher-scholar of White Plains High School, and a man of o'er-weaning virtue. He is known to have thrown "Mush" Goldberg out of a class because a page of his Virgil trot fell out from his text, from which he was reciting aloud while afoot. The trot gave English interlineation to the Latin text. It was a popular illegal learning tool in the 1920's, particularly effective if you were called upon for a quick translation and were unprepared. But its use was banned by Otis Rules. It took a brave man to display a trot before the big eyes of Alvah Tobias Otis who had edited Cicero for the New York State High School Regents Board. His eyes were telescopic, travelled everywhere, and his anger was ferocious. I don't know if "Mush" Goldberg was graduated from White Plains High. I hope he was. Certainly, trot or no trot he was one of the brightest men in our class.

Here I am again in a photograph of the Executive Council standing next to Hayden Goss, who was my nemesis because he stood an inch taller than my 6'5". He jumped center on the basketball team where there was only room for one extra tall person as play was structured at that early time. Tall men jumped center but the rest was for sneaky, fast little guys who came in with scores like 38-22. There right up center is that glorious little girl, Joy Henderson. Her father was a librarian at the 42nd Street Library and she twisted my heart around her pencil; she was pretty, very petite, bright and sweet, but mostly bright. There she stands near the front of the class picture. I am looking at that little girl, hoping that somewhere she is alive and well and has enjoyed the full intelligent life for which she seemed destined. Jane Peters took my heart from this little one, for a short time. A beautiful, artistic young woman, raised mostly in Tientsen as a missionary's daughter, she was soon to be destroyed in an automobile accident, driving home from her first vacation from Oberlin College.

As Editor-in-Chief, I had in 1929-30 run a series of articles in the White Plains High School Orange opposing the fraternity system which at that time controlled the Students' Organization and many of its Social Clubs. These Fraternities for decades were snobbish and aloof. The vast majority of the student body were not fraternity members and so with some friends, we formed the Commons Club and a year later by a large vote, we controlled the Student Government. Our base was egalitarianism and we thought we were speaking for the non-moneyed classes of the high school, i.e., the common man. We were Clintons, nearer in conceptual American time to DeWitt than the President. This political Coup added to an intellectual stance which I was building against institutionalized success. As a freshman at Harvard, I was approached to be pledged by a fraternity, Zeta Beta Tau, which had some standing among college social groups. I rebuffed the solicitor, much to his astonishment, since he had come to me not because he knew me, but because my father was a member of Alpha, the original chapter of ZBT, and my brother had also been a member. It may be pointed out, that about the time I became a Harvard freshman, the House Plan was instituted by the college with its co-mingling of the faculty and students in college residency. The houses eliminated the need for Fraternities which were abandoned by persons with any pretense to sense.

In 1983, at South Newton High School, a very tall, lean, young man gave his Commencement address. He was the Valedictorian. He spoke for peace, expressing frustration and desperation at a World which bristled with stocked Nuclear Arms and needed only a spark to ignite them.

I sat in the auditorium and listened to a strangely persuasive, oratorical voice, which apparently had been passed on to him as it had been passed on to me from some ancient biblical orator. Perhaps from Nathan, the Prophet, who pointed his finger in scorn at the Status Quo and excoriated King David for his abandoned morals. My friend sounded gloomier than I had ever been. He spoke of the disappointed, the fearful, the conquered, all gathered together in holding back the Angel of Death in the form of a nuclear holocaust soon to come, I listened closely to the speaker. He was my grandson, Joshua, and he looked and sounded like me when I was the orator at White Plains High 50 years before.

By 1928 or 1929, a revulsion to war had set in among the young. A shocked public for the first time became aware of how extensively the war government had manipulated the press, and questions arose concerning the values served by World War I. The muck-raking literature about the war had a powerful impact on me and my peers. World War I had been fed by the sinking of the Lusitania, the atrocities of the U-boats on peaceful shipping and the stories of the outrages committed by

German infantrymen as they marched through Belgium and France.

It is December, 1914. My uncle Isaac Newton, the reporter for the New York Times, interviewed Simon Lake in his shipyard offices in Bridgeport Connecticut harbor. Unable to sell his patented submarine to America, Lake did, during the Russo-Japanese War, sell it to the Russian Government. Krupp took over Lake's factory. Krupp then, from the German plant, supplied the Germans as well as the Russians. Lake's ideas, were appropriated by the Germans just before World War I. Simon Lake, whose thinking was the basis for the deadly German submarine that proved to be the scourge of the American and British Merchant Marines, could not sell his ideas to our Navy.

Lord Ponsonby was in charge of British propaganda during the period just before we entered the War in 1917. He wrote of German soldiers mutilating hospital patients in Belgium as they heavy footed it through that little country, and perhaps the most lurid of it was the amputation of the breasts of unfortunate nurses who found themselves in Belgium hospitals when raided by the Germans. After the War, Ponsonby wrote a book called "War Lies" in which he acknowledged that he had made up these stories in order to inflame the Americans. We had our propaganda minister, George Creel, whose acquaintance with the truth by his own admission was largely accidental. When

I read these books, I wrote an indignant column about them in "The Orange", much to the delight of Beverly, our history teacher, who was a "peace monger" in a faculty of "war mongers". In the wake of these revelations came the Oxford oath much circulated in European universities during the late 1920s and which caused many a youngster to swear that he would never go to war under any circumstances. Very rarely, however, when the time came ten years later, did young men keep this oath. I remember as a Harvard College freshman in 1930 learning that it was still circulating for signatures, and several million signatures throughout the world were asserted by the sponsors.

Most of us became pacifists, believing in a world order enforced through world government, supporting the League of Nations which had already become an illusive goal for Americans, and learning the bitter poetry of the war poets of World War I — Sigfried Sassoon, Rubert Hughes, Martin Weinstein: "Eh ho my brother, Jesus, they held you up in state with a gun to tote and a khaki coat; did they think you could learn to hate? Oh, the ranks of the dead go marching by; What can Jesus do but die?"

These moving poems written by soldiers have stuck in my memory since the 1920's. "In Flanders field the poppies grow between the crosses row by row." There was debunking everywhere. The munitions makers were the principal object of scorn, but perhaps nothing else that had been written had more influence on the sophisticated statement of revulsion against war than Shaw's earlier *Major Barbara*. The equities of World War I were not so clear as those found eighteen years later in World War II. The long grim lines of trenches, which served more than anything else as pre-dug graves for thousands of soldiers on each side, made World War I a war of foul means used to accomplish uncertain ends.

World War II became the "good war", in the words of Studs Terkel, and, of course, it is when the Allied victory is assessed against the nightmarish supposition that Hitler had triumphed and much of the world became a charnel house directed by a German madman. And it is not to be supposed that teenage pacifists failed to respond to the threat of Hitler when the threat became known with Hitler's invasion of Austria and Poland. Chamberlain's peace with Hitler was regarded by most college students as a sell out, and many thought the first months of the War with England and France in which there was little action was a "phony War".

At White Plains High School in 1930, I had written in a column in the "Orange" that the proper method of waging War was to have champions struggle in place of armies as Matthew Arnold had described in his epic poem "Sohrab and Rustum" Two great warriors, knowing each other's names, but not the persons to which they attach, served as the great champions of their countries fighting as representatives of their large hosts; they locked in struggle and the younger dying in the older's arms, turned out to be the son of the great Rustum. The symbolism of war represented by father unwittingly slaying his son could not escape even high school students.

The High School paper served as a source of excited debate among students who had differing views as to matters which, whatever their size, loomed big to high schoolers. Everyone tried to write with the sharp wit of George G. Nathan, but none could make it. The faculty, as I recall it , was energetic, and helped stimulate extra-curricular activities and willingly gave of its time, serving as advisors, and often as participants in a world which started after school had ended for the day. There existed an eagerness in-faculty to see child grow into civilized adult state with at least a smidgen of learning, and some contact with the culture of our times. After all, among the subjects we studied were Literature, Latin and Chemistry. It would have been impossible for an illiterate to be graduated from White Plains High School. It is often said that it is not impossible for an illiterate to receive a Bachelors degree from some of our present day colleges, but this is as serious as cigarette-caused cancer or AIDS.

These teachers did not just blot out into the receding sun, but often pushed past the child's innate desire to preserve his status quo of ignorance, and served, I use the word seriously, as stimulators of learning.

A Tip of the Hat to Mr. B.

About 16 years ago, as part of a book put out by Prentice-Hall called "The Teacher", I was asked to do a chapter about the teacher who had the most influence on my thought. I wrote a chapter concerning my high school history teacher who bore the improbable name of Armona C. Beverly. Much of that chapter is contained in the words that follow. But when the book was published in 1967, the publisher thought that if we were interviewed on television it might prove a good advertisement.

I looked for his name in the White Plains directory, hoping for a clue after more than 30 years, and found the name with a Junior attached. I called this person, learned that it was the great Mr. Beverly's son, and was given a phone number in Miami where father could be reached. After sending father a copy of the book and allowing time for him to read it, I called Miami and talked with this great man. "Sure", he said," I read your book, and sure I would like to help, but not now." He said," you see, a few weeks ago I was walking down the boardwalk behind a pretty lady, and soon realized that there was only one rear end like that, and that one was Pinella's, a nurse, with whom I had been madly in love when I was with the AEF in France and she was a World War I nurse. I picked up as much speed as I could — I am 84 years old — caught up with her, and we were soon married. If you think I am going to leave my honeymoon to come up to New York to advertise some book, you are mistaken."

I have come to that age where I ache to find out where I have been; the past has become important—the old joys sometimes glimmer at night, the old pains sometimes throb. From the infinity of memories there lob up good and bad appositions, men and women, the books I have read, and the thousand details of days and nights. But let the mind seek out its influences, and it is the teachers, formal and informal, who stand out.

The school teachers now seem gigantic in their authority, their claims to knowledge, and their eagerness to share it with me. They included the fact men and women: those who went their routine ways trying to project the Latin conjugations, the date and participants in the Treaty of Vienna and the axioms of Euclid. These were the ambient encyclopedias, and the day-laborers of knowledge; most of my teachers are to be counted among them, and, of course, I needed them as much as the police and fire departments, the highways and other public services. Much that they taught me has long been forgotten. But there were a few others, and I was fortunate in viewing a scholarly heaven in which there were pulsating new, bright stars. The names remain clear, the faces, the mannerisms, even some of the words. These were giants holding attitudes of mind valid for an age in which the truth was unattainable, but the search as necessary as food or breath.

I shall ignore the lawmen, the great professors skilled in the ambush of fact and concept: Thomas Read Powell, Felix Frankfurter, Warren Abner Seavey, Zechariah Chafee and many others. My mind was already shaped for good or evil by the time I studied law. There were the college giants: George Lyman Kittredge, Alfred North Whitehead, John Livingston Lowes, Roger Bigelow Merriman, Bernard De Voto—this was a treasure trove of able men, and all shaped and turned my mind like a piece of soft clay.

But behind them loom the real giants, the ones who first showed that the written word was not sacred and that all the millions of words on which the eyes would falter in a lifetime are no more significant than the droppings of pigeons unless they are appraised by a roving and critical brain. They were the first with their cajolery, their wiles, their ruses to implant learning in unenthusiastic young minds. They had the advantage of writing on clean blackboards, of talking first at a time when words would be remembered best, of putting down a mark which would sear itself into the soul.

When Armona C. Beverly taught history at White Plains High School in suburban New York, this was not a school that had made a reputation for training great scholars. If it had fathered any great intellects, we had not been told about them. In 1930 it did send its fair share of graduates to the big universities and they thrived well; It sent to the world automobile mechanics, violinists, college professors satisfying our middle-class destinies as well as other high schools. But I wander from the image of Mr. Beverly.

In 1929 New Rochelle, White Plains' traditional rival, defeated White Plains in football, 45-0. In that year White Plains hired as a coach a professional football player who was paid more than the principal. When the appointment leaked out I wrote an editorial against it in the school paper, "The Orange", but this was not a powerful voice, and for many years thereafter, White Plains enjoyed the doubtful distinction of being invincible in Westchester football. Mr. Beverly anticipated and disliked this eventually, its inappropriateness in a society which already had learned to place too much value upon the unreal and the self-defeating. Beverly referred us to a book by John L. Tunis, a New York Times sports writer—the title has escaped me—which piteously exposed professionalism in collegiate sports. He was with the angels on this and almost every issue, a position which almost always is the minority since, as everyone knows, Hell is more heavily populated than Heaven.

He stood in front of the classroom—large, well-cleaned windows to the left, the corridor door on the right, forty scholars in between, old lithographs of Washington and Lincoln on the wall: I remember that the windows were to my left because "Doll" H— sat next to one and when the sun was strong and her dress thin it was difficult to concentrate on either American or Modern European History. Mr. Beverly had a square Mt. Rushmore-like face, and dryly spoke his skepticism to an audience opening its mind between two wars, at the eve of the depression, but an audience which still held fast to eternal verities: the charm of Greta Garbo, the adventure of a Sabbatini novel, and the concept that even the meanest among us might one day be president.

When the papers reveled in the veniality of Jimmie Walker, Mr. Beverly felt no surprise. He recommended Lincoln Steffens' *The Shame of the Cities* to the point that corruption was the expectable norm in the management of big cities. The presence of our marines in Nicaragua caused Mr. Beverly to assign Scott Nearing's *Dollar Diplomacy*. That was pretty stiff going in our little Republican town. I have not seen the book since, but I remember it saddened us with its talk of American imperialism in Latin America; we were proud of Wilson and what he called the "New Freedom," but Muzzey's *History of the American People* taught us that we had imposed a Pax Americana upon Latin America. We believed in our freedom, and we thought that there must be moral content in public matters, particularly in the movement of our troops. Mr. Beverly led us little by little to a point of view that was ready to question anything, and regarded nothing as a "sacred cow."

Mr. Beverly stood in front of the room, a firm pillar of righteousness, challenging the falsehoods of man, both public and private. His heroes were Jefferson, Lincoln and Theodore Roosevelt. He asked whether the United States had ever waged aggressive war, a challenging question to the dewy-eyed innocents of 1930; to the outraged negative he replied with a description of President Lincoln's "Spot Resolutions." Lincoln in Congress challenged the statement of President Polk that Mexico had started the war by first spilling American blood on American soil. "Show us the spot," the indignant Lincoln had cried out, and so more than 90 years later did Mr. Beverly, as we all cringed in our chairs feeling the collective guilt of the Mexican war.

This heresy proved a little too much for the staid editor of *The White Plains Daily Reporter*, the local molder of the public opinion, which was willing to enter political controversy provided it was a century old. It doubted whether Mr. Beverly was suited to his teaching position, and suggested that the local Superintendent of Schools conduct an inquiry. We had learned too much to let the matter alone. A number of us traipsed down to the Superintendent's office and were among the angels speaking for Mr. B., who was vindicated on more important grounds than our testimony. Indeed, the trip was unnecessary, since the Superintendent had disposed of the complaint summarily.

I remember writing a good, sound sixteen-year-old's letter to the "Open Forum" column of *The Reporter*, which was first acknowledged by an editorial explaining why the paper would not engage in editorial debate with a high school boy, and then said that if I would identify myself, the letter would be printed. Over the vault of years, I remember well that it was printed with a typographical error in almost every line.

I do not hesitate any longer to say that I was one of Mr. B.'s favorites. It comes to me now that I sat near the front, and one morning was contemplating the historical verities while munching a Milky Way, badly hidden behind my spiral notebook. "Hoffmann" bellowed Mr. B., "This is not the cafeteria. Leave the room at once and don't return until you have finished eating." And then, with a great show of anger, he followed me down the aisle and out the door into the corridor. "Give me half," he said, "I'm starving."

I have read great books and known great teachers. My mind has lumbered through a large and important period of American history that has swirled on with me on this uncertain planet. I do not pretend to have understood what has happened since I left White Plains High, but I have accepted little that was pre-cooked for me and thought more about the bases of my faith because of Mr. Beverly. When he gave us Mencken he gave us a scalpel and not a bomb. He did not leave us in despair but in confidence that free inquiry is a national asset. He loved our egalitarian national dream, but made us familiar with Goldsmith's happy phrase, "A citizen of the world." More than anything else we learned to partake of skeptical, pragmatic inquiry, in my view America's most lasting contribution to this generation's civilization. We were bathed in freedom's dream, and held that nothing was unobtainable to a searching mind in this land where the Indian trails climb over huge snow-capped mountains, and the prairie lands sweep their rich fields farther than you and I can travel in three days in a Model A Ford.

Mr. Beverly, to you I tip the derby hat we seniors wore in 1930.

A.F.H.

I f you think of me, having read thus far, as a sober, sensitive man who can recognize "hard facts" when in their presence, I shall ask that you skip this little section entitled A.F.H.[*], lest you learn the truth, which is that I believe that there is not much difference between the real and make believe. That hard facts are soft facts, and that if you are a poet you can go through life making poetry of your experiences. I believe, also, in relation to people, that each person is many people, one of whom may be attracted to another's least representative personality like iron filings to the ends of a magnet. Perhaps you can test the existence of love by the circumstance that one would find it impossible to write something bad about the other. That is romantic nonsense, but that is the way it was between me and A.F.H

The images formed by computers are still more or less featureless and give the impression of quick

---

[*] A.F.H. is shorthand for Anna Frances Hoffmann.

moving rectangular life. In a sense this is true abstractionism, the reduction of humankind to pulsating geometric forms. Moreover, the computer memory is long on facts and short on beauty. If, as Professor Maisky believes, we shall become pets in a park run by computers, the chances are that we will not be selected for kindly treatment because of our beauty either of the spirit or the flesh. Perhaps computer approval will come to those who best can handle mathematics, or are best coordinated between eye and hand. But I think of women in full human dimensions.

In the world of long ago I first saw Anna sitting with my aunt Rebecca in a 1932 Chevrolet, at a subway exit in the Inwood Section of Manhattan. The year was 1935 and I was arriving to spend my Christmas vacation at my aunt's school away from the arduous duties of a first year law student at the Harvard Law School. The two ladies sat side by side. My aunt with a square jaw and penetrating eyes had her mouth curled in the pleasure of recognition as I came out of the subway. Next to her I realized with almost a physical start were two of the largest and shiest and most limpid sky blue eyes that I have ever seen. They rested in a face beautifully Italian in the imperial sense. One did not have to talk with her to realize that this was a great lady whose portrait the best Italian artists had sought after for the last 500 years. Our ride was only a few blocks to a great red brick building which lodged the Hoffmann School and where my new found lady was assisting my aunt by teaching the kindergarten. I knew almost at the first glance that I was in serious trouble because her face and manner expressed not only the presence of a beautiful woman confident in her beauty but also suggested a spirit shaping her thoughts and actions which had to be reckoned with on some different level from the ordinary relationships of new found friends. She came from Brooklyn, New York, and from a neighborhood which was generally accepted as a suburb of Rome. Her father owned a marble factory. Her mother sat back in the lonely glory of a Sicilian woman who did not deign to master the language of the new country even more than 40 years after her arrival there as a young girl.

Although she had a sizable family, it was quite enough that there was Anna and from the first minute on when I talked to her I sensed I was already enmeshed in a Herculean struggle which might result in the loss of my bachelorhood. She was 5'2" tall but stood in such a way as to suggest that she was 5'4", an altitude to which she made some unconvincing claim. Anna always appeared to be an extraordinary figure to the children or parents who came under her supervision or sought her advice in the 43 years remaining of her life, during most of which she directed the Hoffmann School. A Lincoln when asked said that a man's legs should be long enough to reach the ground. She was 21 years old then and had just been graduated from an experimental branch of Teachers' College. She was already confirmed in her profession of early childhood education. I was still a student, although only three weeks younger than this mature lady. That Christmas holiday Anna had undertaken to stay with my aunt in order to offer supervision for some of the children in the Boarding Department who could not go home for a holiday.

I was now subject to the persuasive power of propinquity. For ten days or so the girl next door slept in the room below me and my desires and affection were fanned by the sharing of meals together and the numerous other meetings necessary when living together in the same house. Within a few days I invited her to a movie—"As You Like It" with Elizabeth Bergner—which was showing at a great neon lighted theatre fittingly called "Paradise" on the Grand Concourse and Fordham Road in the Borough of the Bronx. Near to it was the one-time home of Edgar Allan Poe and near to that was a tavern bearing Poe's name. In that tavern my demure new friend ordered ginger ale and I, to display my machismo, six tankards of beer which I lined up in a row. I disposed of the beer to her astonishment and somewhat to her distaste. Also, she reminded me later, I recited Poe's "Raven" from "Once upon a midnight dreary" onto its dreary end, the last "nothing more" coinciding with the last drop of beer in Cyrano style. This I did in my best oratorical manner with grand cadence and accentuated rhyme.

I told her that Elizabeth Bergner was my great passion and that I would cross the world for her. And with considerable exaggeration I described Ms. Bergner's prowess as an actress. This actress, if my memory serves me well, was very tiny and spoke English with a continental accent. Leslie Howard was also in the same version of "As You Like It," a fact of more interest to my charming lady. I remember hearing later on that Leslie Howard, who more than any actor, came to epitomize John Bull was born in Budapest and had never spoken a word of English until he was 18 years of age. As Shaw observed in "Pygmalion", the truest English is spoken by a trained foreigner. I remember hearing also that David Ross who for many years, was the finest radio announcing voice working for CBS radio and year after year received a prize for best enunciation and diction, was a European refugee who reached adulthood with a heavy Yiddish accent. Somebody remarked to him as he read poetry aloud in Village boites that he would be a wonderful radio announcer if only he spoke better English. He then went to language school and learned to speak the purest English in town with the possible exception of Milton Cross who was his counterpart at NBC. Art sometimes conquers nature.

I consumed beer and later with my last 50 cents I took her back to the school in a taxicab, observing that I did not like subways and for the rest of my life I proposed to use taxicabs. Of this, too, Anna reminded me later when it had become my destiny that I rarely travelled in any way other than cab.

I was showing off to the best of my ability, serving some ideogram of mine as a brilliant, poetical young man. My shirt collar was open in the fashion I thought common to Edgar Allan Poe and Lord Byron, and I sensed that I looked a little wan but strong, a figure who might appeal to more than one instinct of an impressionable young woman. Many years later she told me that I did my work well since by the time we returned to the school she had set her cap for me and it would have gone badly for me if our romance had not taken place.

By the next holiday I saw her in action as a school teacher and realized that this was an extraordinary young woman. Her classroom tingled with a kind of warm excitement; and she played the piano as her little students swarmed around her piano and all participated in that great learning experience of identification of notes and chords. She sat on the floor of the classroom painting with the children and always encouraging them; one could appreciate immediately that there was a love bond between her and each child in the room. A well known educator, Helen Parkhurst, founder of the Dalton Plan, described it to me many years later. She said,

"It was a mother-teacher-child chain of confidence. I have seen it only twice in many decades of educational work, once with Anna Hoffmann and once with Ilona Montessori." When Anna died in 1980 after having run the Hoffmann School for some 35 years, expressions of grief came to me from all over the world, from students now middle aged who had had no contact with the school for 20 or 30 years.- The story was always the same, "I loved her and I got my early childhood education because I would have followed her anywhere and did, even to learning how to read, write and do arithmetic." A college student wrote saying he owed everything to her. This young man, the son of an accomplished physician and a great advertising woman, had been told by a local Riverdale school which was expert in the fields of arrogance and snobbery, that he was dull and would get nowhere and should learn a trade. His parents brought the child to Anna for testing. She spent several hours with him, announced that he was a perfectly normal boy, capable of the same achievement as his brothers and sisters. She took in to the school a lad of 9 or 10 who was terrified by fake English style education, had no confidence in his ability to succeed, and had been so discouraged by the predecessor school that he made no effort to accomplish anything, avoiding defeat by withdrawing from the battle. The young man now a college junior, wrote of this to me in a letter and said: "She gave me my manhood by conveying to me in several ways the information that I was as good as my classmates and that I should always reach out farther than I believed possible."

Just as in the Shalom Aleichem story the prosecuting angel for the first time declined to prosecute when Bunchie Schweig came before him, so, too, the angel must have declined again when Anna appeared before him. During the last 5 years of her life she continued to run her school while her body experienced removal of some of her organs under the surgeon's knife. She never protested, she did not cry and even the horrors of chemotherapy which sometimes caused her to be bedridden for days never caused a complaint, never once did she articulate the question, "Why me?". Finally, I sat at her side in a hospital room holding her hand, that very soft hand which tried to grip mine but could only apply a little pressure for lack of strength. I held her hand until it dropped from mine and I saw a smile on her face which suggested that she was being joyously welcomed in some other world than ours.

I cannot find now the verbal versatility which would be necessary faithfully to describe her career or our love.

I have taken upon myself to present a phenomenon of nature in a few words for eyes which will not believe and persons who cannot know, no matter what my words, the phenomenon which I describe.

I was with this selfless woman from 1937 to 1980. As best she could, she provided companionship, encouragement, and material aid to four or five members of her own family and to numerous friends and students at her school. Not given to many words, she chose the ones she used for full effect, leaving no room for debate around the edges of an idea. When a change of importance to our lives was before us, she would ask, "Shall we do it?" rather than anguish through the details of argument. If my answer was "yes", that was an end to it, without the necessity for a long exposition as to why it was the right choice. Only when there was a difference between us, was there debate, and she could be counted on in such debate to place her choices in the squares of good feeling, warm compassion, the beautiful, the loving, and the kind. For many years, she declined to wear a fur coat. Not to protect the animals, but because a school director with children around her doesn't wear a fur coat, even if her husband can provide it.

She rarely sought out elaborate restaurants because her sense of good food and how it is prepared led her away from such irrelevancies as grand ambiance and affected manners of serving.

She liked serious theatre, but mostly she liked beauty in the theatre, as with the ballet company Sadler Wells. She was captivated by some of the effects at the Metropolitan Opera, such as the forest scenes of Marc Chagall in "The Magic Flute".

She could not bear to watch television without accomplishing something useful at the same time, and it was before the television set that she produced her beautiful objects of needlepoint.

She noticed sunsets and day breaks. She stood often before our window, with its large expanse of Hudson River before it, and watched shimmering sunsets and color patterns around the edges of the Palisades.

Her love for children was intense. Her face would light up with the sound of a distant child, even if there was no further contact with it. The love she offered me was unending. She was mother and wife on the grand scale, at the same time devoting maximum energy to her school and faculty and the students in it. This is all a conclusionary statement, but for the details of four and a half decades of this lady's life, a book of different purpose and interest is required.

She, and I, too, were both star-lit visitors from outer space. We felt that neither of us need accept fully the grim reality that we live in a society where one must work for money. She ran a school for about 100 children for over 35 years, all four seasons of the years, nights running into days, living with her parents' and children's concerns and the most she ever took out from the school as money in a single year was $3,800, but generally she took nothing at all and often it was my duty to make up a deficit out of the proceeds of my law practice. Her work was for children and she thought that she was in the direct line of fire in the war against civilization. She said that if the children could not achieve, were not strongly motivated, then our civilization was failing more surely than through outright destruction by warfare. Though most use their memories and some intelligence they must also develop good work habits, they must utilize their lives effectively, but mostly they must walk on this strange planet with a sense of wonder.

The school would be over by 4 p.m. and my wife quickly shifted into her motherly capacity. Our two little girls climbed the stairs together with their mother, the director, and on entering our apartment, shut the door with the knowledge that school was over and that from this time on they were at home. These little girls grew beautifully. Both had the sense of wonder; both yearned not only to share in the accomplishments of our civilization but also to walk proudly on the earth and to laugh at the great comedy of manners and social interrelationships and to cry with the great tragedy of deprival, and they grew to be educated, happy persons with fine careers in their own right and children and husbands who love them.

But along about 7 p.m. I would arrive either from my job in the United States Courthouse at Foley Square, 12 miles away, which I held from 1944-1955 or later on from my private law office in midtown Manhattan. I was, almost without exception, greeted by a wife who appeared as if she had nothing to do all day but beautify herself and two young ladies eager to enter into the delights of dinner, which included, in addition to the great works of a fabulous chef-wife, such verbal activities as "Stinky Pinky," or telling a story around the table, each person adding something to the description and movement of plot given by the person ahead; moving plots sometimes developed like coral reefs. We talked of school, the peculiarities and atrocities of teachers and, at an appropriate age, we freely considered the merits and demerits of the boys or young men who were pursuing our daughters. We talked of the news and made puns and jokes and, as the children grew into their teens, they developed a lively interest in music, painting and other arts.

My younger daughter, Jessica, talented in story-telling and painting, developed a liking for the guitar and sang together in our living room with Carly Simon, the latest songs learned from radio or television. Even though Carly became one of the greatest of our professional dramatic singers, this couple frequently drove me from the room since I maintained a parental disapproval of guitars and the tight jeans of thirteen year old girls, neither of which I dared articulate. Sometimes in the evenings, Ruth Lipscomb, who had been a concert pianist and was the music director of Hoffmann School, would stay and play four hands with

Trudy, my elder daughter, or Ruth would entertain us with the sweetest use of a piano I knew. On a few occasions, Ruth came to dinner accompanied by her old friend, Mary Lou Williams, whose mastery of jazz, has placed her among our greatest musicians. The upright almost jumped to their magnificent 20 fingers. Ruth and Mary Lou had dark skins and so, too, had many others who were on staff at my wife's school. Anna was born color-blind and also born a democrat in the true sense of the word because she lived out our democracy with her life, her school's policies, and her inability to become a snob. She often forgave tuition payments (de facto scholarships) because she could not think of tuition as money, but as a ticket for the improvement of life. She loved almost all the children who ever entered in her school. Her office was well equipped with Band-Aids and lollipops and there was no requirement to keep out. Here a 5-year old could call his mother and complain of the latest indignity in life, or my wife held to her bosom someone who that day no longer was able to grapple with the demands of others.

Enough of this, I say that her 35 years as head of Hoffmann School is a life rebuttal to the materialistic drang of the century and for thousands of children who were touched by her wand, a demonstration of the living democracy.

Harvard: The First Four Years

1930–1934

I had no roommate when, in September 1930, I first arrived at the Harvard campus; the boy I had hoped I would room with was at the last minute refused admission. Thus, when I arrived in Cambridge and went to the Bursar's office, a then modern red brick building called Lehman Hall, I was given an assignment to Clavery Hall, a cold, old Gold Coast dormitory. Its ceilings and walls were matted by burlap coverings, slightly dusty and gloomy, but characteristic of a no longer lamented, turn-of-the-century decor. I was 6'-6" tall, had a glossy new black trunk, a huge old suitcase loaned by an aunt festooned with European hotel labels, and I was very much afraid.

I remember an old brown leather sofa with some of the stuffing pushing out of its rounded edges. I remember the provenance of a continuous red brick wall seen through the window; my suite seemed as far removed from my world of warmth and friendship as a vacant igloo.

In a very few days I went to the Bursar's office and asked that I be assigned a roommate. Another lonely freshman was found on Lehman Hall records. It was thus that I met Marty Mercer and the two of us shared rooms on the fifth floor of Apley Court, another Gold Coast dormitory, but this was suffused with light, and opposite a newly constructed gymnasium which I rarely used; but whose presence served to twinge my conscience. I was sedentary then and am now six decades later.

Martin Mercer was 6'-1" tall, eighteen years of age and spoiled beyond all possibility of redemption.

Marty was a sadist and the possessor of most of the known currency west of the Atlantic ocean. At a time when we were all without funds because the depression held the land in its dark fist, Marty had money to spare. He delighted to dispense with it through the process of offering his classmates "dares."

One rainy night Marty challenged four of us walking across the quad behind Elliot house, to mount and remain until morning on an outside sundial, which stood free of all surrounding trees and buildings and was the subject of the wrath of the wind and the rain. One of my friends, equipped with poncho and rainhat, climbed the sundial and said that Marty's dare in the amount of $10 was taken—a sheik's ransom in 1931. We soon dispersed, leaving a forlorn Marty and his victim standing in the rain at about one in the morning. Some minutes later, Marty returned to our suite, announcing with considerable pleasure that our friend on the sundial was so uncomfortable that he could not last very much longer. Marty then promptly went to sleep. Marty's sleep was not performed in quite the same way as it is by the rest of mankind or even by certain canines who, before sleeping, revolve in a counterclockwise direction in order to insure that there is no enemy present.

Marty slept flat on his back. It was often difficult to know whether he was in fact asleep, or whether the edge of his eyes which emerged from under his lids were in fact perceiving the world around him. The normal run of mankind just doesn't crack knuckles in its sleep. Sometimes I was awakened by the cracking sound and saw Marty sitting on his bed, cracking his knuckles merrily, but snoring simultaneously. That fateful night, Marty cracked his knuckles until 4:00 a.m. and when morning came, the rain still was with us. Out of the rainstorm, at about 9:00 a.m., emerged a wet and bedraggled figure, demanding that Marty at once pay over $10. Marty took the position, which might have had some foundation in the logic of Thomas Aquinas and other deductive thinkers, that our friend could not have spent the night on the sundial—the storm was too great for that, the rain too plentiful. Our friend, however, whose wily ways later won him a judgeship in the District of Columbia, would have none of this. He stated firmly, bringing home to Marty the fact that he meant business, "You will never know, will you, whether or not I sat on the sundial all night? All you have is my word for it." The discussion went along the lines that Marty did not trust the word of our friend and was reluctant to part with $10 on insufficient evidence. Our friend, however, made the point, and I thought it a cunning one, that if Marty did not part with the $10 on the spot, he would soon receive lacerations on both cheeks and possibly a broken jaw. It is then that Marty paid the money and I learned some lesson about the law of evidence: direct testimony, even if self-serving, is better than mere speculation.

Mercer was a millionaire's son and lived on Park Avenue in New York City in a duplex apartment. That apartment had a library of great size with shelves laden with Morocco-tooled volumes including a priceless leather bound set of Shakspere with profuse hand-painted illustrations. On the first visit to the Mercer establishment in New York, I had the temerity to remove for curiosity one of the Shakspere's from the shelf in order to admire it. My roommate put a stop to such nonsense. He explained to me that the books in this library which his father had acquired were not to be read, but were "collectors items" containing hand painted illustrations. I remember well, even now, that there was at one end a faintly lighted window with a stained glass image of Falstaff gamboling with some of the merry wives of Windsor.

During the first few months of our life together, Marty succeeded in introducing me to cigarettes which were passed around by the makers free in great numbers in the shadows of Harvard Yard. It was common to walk to the yard, look for some Lucky Strike or Chesterfield salesman, and receive again and again and again in the course of the day, little packets with four cigarettes designed to induce the student to form a worthwhile lifetime habit. Mine lasted thirty years. By the time I emerged from seven years in Cambridge, I smoked three packs a day and often had two cigarettes lit at once. An elite education can be lost in smoke.

Marty developed a new enthusiasm at the frequency of about one every two weeks, but it was generally accompanied by some superb new possession which took up space in our suite. First he bought a record player with a remarkable device for 1931, the Garrard record changer. This picked up the edge of the record with silvery fingers and turned the record over so that the second side could be played immediately following the first side. It also picked up the next record in the same way, and thus you could play records indefinitely, marred only by the occasional grunting of the machine. No one knew the cost of this device, but it was believed to be enough to buy Holland. Either in connection with this extravagance or some other, Marty announced that he had no difficulty in getting funds from his mother, because he knew of a trip she had taken to Lake Louise with a strange gentleman unknown to her husband.

Marty seemed not to feel that there was any evil involved in blackmailing his mother, nor did he seem to have any sense of value judgment which led him to believe that anything he did was wrong.[1] I thought that he was an imp of good fortune because no one ever seemed really to upend him. He regarded the Harvard curriculum as something to be avoided, but only so far avoided as successfully could be done while still getting passing grades. He regarded all output of energy as being contrary to some universal law of nature, and his typical position was seated in a soft chair which featured a movable back allowing him to recline with arms outstretched in a simulation of death.

He had a loud voice which could be heard on spring nights far from our room and his pursuit of such concerns as bathtub gin and night games of poker were very disconcerting to a serious roommate. I would study in my bedroom but the closed door could not block out the din. Our suite, like almost all of that era, consisted of two bedrooms with a common room between them. Marty's insistent voice seemed to occupy the whole suite and operated as a substitute for thought.

---

[1] Marty is a somewhat fictitious, unknown and unbelievable person, not living nor dead.

Once he bought a motion picture camera and projector and make-up kit and produced his own version of Dr. Caligari, in which an innocent, decent citizen is transformed into a monster with huge, fang-like teeth. These teeth cost $.20 in a store which had theatrical oddities. At the onset of death, the monster resumes his innocent mien. Needless to say, Marty played Dr. Caligari and I played the monster, and the scene in which the transformation took place was a remarkable bit of pictorial ingenuity. First, Marty insisted that my face be powdered white. And then, as I lay on the floor with my theatrical fangs sticking out, he took pictures at strange angles and followed them by a gradual transformation which was achieved by removing one piece of theatrical make-up after another, while taking pictures episodically. For example, heavy, bushy eyebrows had been pasted down. He took off one and shot some film and then took off the other and shot some more. As the film ended, I lay there in total innocence with my normal, handsome face in a blissful smile of death.

Marty's dares were legion, and they may have constituted an altruistic method of transferring money from his ample treasury to the limited treasuries of his friends, although I think that this is too charitable an interpretation. On the occasion he offered his usual $5, (bear in mind that in 1930-31-32, $5 was at least the equivalent of $50 today) to a friend of ours who was about the same weight as Marty, but was of lighter financial means. He was to carry Marty from the first floor of Apley court, up four flights, to the fifth floor where we lived. The flights were steep. The stairway, and the din which accompanied this heroic event, compelled the presence of almost all residents of Apley Court—clamoring up the marble stairs, urging on their hero in the desperate task of carrying Marty from the lowest rung to the top. Our hero paused at each landing, puffing mightily, but Marty would not get off his shoulders to permit rest. Our hero would lean against the wall, utter grandiloquent freshman oaths and then carry on for another flight of stairs. Presently, Marty was carried almost to the top, but a rung or two below he jumped off our hero's shoulders and said, "I withdraw my offer." Thus, in my first year in Harvard College, without the slightest premonition that I would go to Harvard Law School, I learned something about a unilateral contract, which for its consummation calls for performance of an act.

It may be noted that the combined effort of the group completed performance. Marty was forcibly put back on our hero's shoulders, who, like an N.F.L. ball-carrier, busted his way over the two steps. It was quite clear that if Marty had failed to pay the $5, he would have been in the hands of a lynching mob.

As his roommate, and a scholarship boy almost without funds, I was frequently subject to Marty's dares. I remember one; drink a Coca-Cola glass full of Castor Oil. I politely declined. I remember another which was to climb down a rope ladder that probably had not been used for forty years, down the side of our building from the fifth floor to the sidewalk. This offer was declined impolitely. I did, however, accept, on a winter's day, the following terms and conditions, all for $5 in very valuable hard currency. I must sit in the bathtub for three minutes in very cold water. I thought this through and armed myself with several sweaters, heavy underwear, old trousers, ski socks, sneakers and the like in order to face the cold water of mid-winter in Cambridge, Massachusetts. Marty, in his turn, opened up all the windows of our suite, turned off the radiators and ran water in the tub for at least twenty minutes to make sure that it was at it's maximum freeze. And it was a bleak, freezing winters day. I sat in the tub, giving Marty his money's worth, issuing cries of anguish from time to time and carefully looking at my watch, knowing full well that if I were two seconds short in leaving the tub, Marty would say the contract had not been performed. I came to the end of the allotted time and jumped out quickly and shed my clothing, toweling myself off and felt none the worse for wear. Marty, however, by this time seemed to have lost his enthusiasm for the game. I suspect he was experiencing a chill. He had apparently forgotten that in the course of exposing me to the cold water under the most frigid of conditions, including windows wide open, he would be subject to the same climate as I except for the water. That night I hung my soaked long johns out the window to dry. Next morning they stood erect by themselves, some six feet of underwear frozen solid stiff. An old college chum remembers shaking hands with them the next morning.

There was a popular comic cartoon that appeared in the Boston papers, which projected a character with a long overcoat sweeping the floor; he wore a derby hat over his ears. He would knock at a door under comic conditions and always ended his remarks with, "Benny sent me." One evening when Marty mused about some interesting thing that might be done to perforate his quiescent boredom, in through the door plunged a mutual friend, Phil Ranger. Phil was a frail lad of medium height and Marty's ingenious brain took him in all at once; and in one of those moments experienced only by such as Edison and Einstein, Marty said to Ranger—"$5 if you take Hoffmann's overcoat and derby hat and ride through the subway to Boston and back, saying, if anybody makes comments, 'Benny sent me.'"

Ranger was not loath to receive $5, making it part of his condition of performance that Marty pay up front. Ranger returned later, somewhat tipsy, saying that his mission was fulfilled, and reported that as he turned around to pay his second subway fare back from Boston, some Harvard upperclassmen engaged him in conversation in which they pretended to know Benny. It seems that these newly made friends were headed for the Copley Plaza which boasted a rather ornate circular, slowly moving bar, where some of the best Brahmins and other superior forms of Boston life could be found by evening getting looped. Ranger reported that he had a great deal of difficulty in obtaining service because of his strange attire. He was accepted because only a Harvard man would dress like that and what is better than a Harvard man?

As the freshman year ended, I anticipated eagerly life in the House Plan which was a complex of dormitories, some of them new, some reconstructed, designed to simulate to some extent life at the separate colleges of Oxford and Cambridge. These houses, available then to upperclassmen, presented new, educational concepts, which were fulfilled only partly. One was to create a more intimate relationship between faculty and student by the requirement that a number of tutors and younger faculty people live within the rooms of the houses. There was a large common room at Kirkland House and a formal dining room, vestige of a splendid old freshman dorm called Smith Hall. One could, if he made an effort, find himself at the same table at dinner with a faculty member, or even enter conversation with one in a common room. Such activity was not altogether popular among the undergraduates. The House Plan also provided splendid libraries in each of the houses, as well as limited athletic facilities.

The Houses were not, however, places where classes were held, nor did they replace the functions of the administration nor the lecture halls that were lodged in the Harvard Yard itself. It was said that the House Plan resulted from a very sizeable gift flowing from a philanthropist named Harkness, who was a Yale graduate and originally had offered the idea of the House Plan to Yale. This gift, apparently was turned down by some anglophobic administrator, but eagerly accepted by President Lowell of Harvard, who was nonpareil in discharging the presidential function of fund raising and who talked persuasively in the Boston style of a British accent.

Later, after the Harvard buildings were erected and the plan established, Harkness made a similar now acceptable gift to his repentant alma mater.

I found myself applying for space in the New Houses. In their beginnings, the space was not quite adequate to house all undergraduates. It was then that Marty came to me and urged that we apply for space together. My sense of caution said "no," but I was not yet at a stage of life when I could refuse when the refusal was reproach. By this time, Marty had reached totally ambivalent status in my affections. I thought of him as a sympathetic character; a poor little rich boy who had been deprived of a decent bringing up, but at the same time he symbolized to my mind what was the worst in our upper-middle class milieu. He was a handsome young man, given to social living and desirable to a long list of princesses in the nearby women's colleges. He, also, as this recital suggests, was almost totally amoral, except in the area of social taboos. Let me put it this way, with the advantage of hindsight, I certainly would never have permitted a daughter of mine to go out with him. Marty was, however, regarded by many eligible young women, and their parents as well, as what was then called a "catch".

Thus, I found myself residing with Marty in Kirkland House, doomed to a second year with a flamboyant, noisy, but often genial friend. Later on, he shared space with a former Exeter classmate of his, who was a fabulously intense scholar, and of whom it was said that while Marty was conducting a party he could sit in the same room and prepare for the next day's classes without the slightest awareness of what Marty and his friends were doing. This extraordinary concentration enabled Marty's new roommate to rise high in the ranks of industry in later life, but I cannot report that my concentrative powers were so good as his.

Flip recollections of friends and amusements in no way express the meaning of the Harvard experience. Straight out of White Plains High School, and the conqueror of the world at White Plains

High School, I was overwhelmed by life and learning in Cambridge, Massachusetts. I started with a scholarship given by Price Greenleaf, who made it part of the grant that the beneficiary work a few hours for Harvard University. I was given a job at University Hall writing little blurbs for the newspapers concerning the appointments of professors, faculty books, new achievements of the university, etc. Professor Hooton, a physical anthropologist, had written a book with a recondite title: "Harvard Men Are Growing Heavier and Taller." I weighed 180 pounds as a freshman, but had grown almost taller than everyone and was 6'-6" high at the age of eighteen and never to grow any higher, although from time to time, I worried that I might spurt up some more and become a circus giant. These were the days when not more than one or two of the basketball players on the team were more than 6' tall.

Hooton's book was based on anthropometric statistics which Harvard had started to collect before the Revolutionary War. Hooton also had access to army statistics from various wars through World War I and came up with the startling conclusion that second generation Harvard men were the second tallest group of men in the world, averaging about 6'-1" tall, exceeded only by the Watusi, who averaged well over 6'-4". If my memory is correct, he attributed Harvard heights to a good diet and plenty of opportunity for children to play outdoors.

He pointed to the remarkable growth of children of immigrants, particularly from the Mediterranean area, who, when exposed to the American diet and baseball, became as tall as everybody else. I did not find this statistical demonstration as persuasive as it would seem because of its arbitrariness. His generalizations left no room for me, whose father was 6'-3" and grandfather was said to be 6'-7", the latter raised in Moscow, Russia.

The Harvard catalogue for the early 1930s shows a wealth of courses in classical, literary and philosophical fields as well as much history and government as anyone could desire. Language courses were available in Chinese and Japanese, Aramaic, Syriac, Indic philology and Egyptian. The college in the early 1930s was on the rebound from the permissive, gentlemanly life of the late '20s, the age of affluence and the John Held cartoon, the short skirts, the raccoon coats and ever-multiplying football stadia.

Harvard at least had established ferocious academic standards. It was not at all uncommon for first year college students to flunk out, and freshman from small high schools like mine were not entirely confident that they could compete successfully with the graduates of Exeter and Andover who were liberally represented in our classes. I was, however, a reader of books, not only from my school life, but because of reading habits early formed. It was not unusual for me to read two novels in the course of one evening, consuming perhaps as many as 800 or 900 pages at a very fast reading rate which stayed with me until I went to Harvard Law School and began the baffling procedure of reading law cases, a process which slowed my reading forever. Most of the books I read in college had not been assigned as part of the curriculum and I enjoyed a sense of abandon in selecting my reading at Widener Library which made most of the writings of the world readily available. In my sophomore year I found that Kirkland House had a small library in a Revolutionary War framed house called Hicks House. One could find a quiet musty corner there in a small room and read until the library closed at 10 o'clock without seeing another soul and with a sense of being engulfed by the great words and sentiments of the great giants of the mind who had walked the world for so many generations.

Perhaps, too often I read the poets because I enjoyed the lilt and sound of the words and was aided by a quick memory which often enabled me to recite a dozen lines or more on two or three quick readings. I would sometimes walk around the campus reciting what I had just read in order to fixate it in my memory where some of it has lingered half a century.

I chose English literature as my field of concentration. The college attempted to help freshmen make their decisions as to majors which would be operative at the start of their second year by presenting introductory courses in different fields and by descriptive literature. The college was aware that a freshman could not make a very informed choice of subject matters; Professor Chester Noyes Greenough saying, "The man who cannot read the bill of fare may get something to eat, but he cannot be said to have chosen his courses." An effort was made to require some knowledge of matters other than the field of concentration such as the requirement for a course in science or math, and in the field of history, government and economics. The choice between mathematics or science led me to take a geology course given by Professor Kirtly B. Mather. It pushed the imagination. The student was required to think in terms of huge masses, partly or totally obscured by the flow of time measured by millions of years. It brought home the smallness of man in a total life process.

As to English, in the study of particular authors such as Shakspere and Milton, it was the objective, according to Professor John Tatlock, for the faculty to read with the students the accurate texts of literary works. "No rapid reading of Shakspere plays privately can take the place of proceeding step by step through Shakspere's very lines and words with the help of one who knows the poet intimately."

And so I found myself sitting in English II, George Lyman Kittredge's course in Shakspere where in one entire year we tussled line by line through six of the great plays. We read by ourselves the rest of the thirty-seven during a reading period lasting three weeks or so at the end of the semester. I learned that when Shakspere used the word "let" it did not mean to permit or to rent, but meant to "bar" or "prevent." We used little red one volume texts which had been prepared by a former student of Kittredge named William J. Rolfe who had been headmaster at the Cambridge high School. His texts were sprinkled with most of the erudition in the field in long notes in the back of the texts. Between the pages I applied transparent onion sheets with gummed edges, a popular Harvard learning tool, and on this day by day I recorded the word by word comments by Professor Kittredge in going through each play. Kittredge dominated the classroom with a sense of majesty which it was hard for any professor to rival. He and George Bernard Shaw were look alikes and one story reports that they once sat in boxes at opposite sides of Covent Garden. An observer said to Kittredge, "you look just like Shaw." "No," Kittredge replied, severely, "Shaw looks like me."

The stories about Kittredge were legion. My favorite has to do with Kittredge's insistence that students be in the classroom ready for his lecture by five minutes after the hour. On one occasion he approached the lectern and spied a student still settling down in his seat. He went on a tirade against unmannerly students, ending with a per-oration which sounded something like, "I don't know what has happened to manners. Your fathers would never have dared to be late contrary to their professor's instructions." He glowered at the young man who had just settled himself. And then in a final ecstasy of rage, the professor said, addressing the young man directly, "You will not be permitted to participate this hour. Leave the room." The young man picked up from the floor beneath his yellow seat, two crutches and with great difficulty started to rise from his seat. He had been a victim of infantile paralysis, the scourge of young people in the first half of the century. Kittredge's imperious head took in this scene. Suddenly tears came to his crusty eyes and he said, "Please sit down young man. Sometimes I fail to remember that a professor must have good manners." Harvard graduates who viewed Kittredge as an imperturbable rock will scarcely believe the story, but I was there and it happened in my class. It was also said of Kittredge that he declined to stand for a Ph.D., observing that he did not know of anyone on the Harvard faculty capable of giving him the examination.

Another Kittredge episode, and this is the last, had to do with a Radcliffe girl taking Kittredge's course. She quarreled with his pronunciation of a word. He arbitrarily put her down. The next day she toted into the classroom a huge Webster's International Dictionary which bore out her statement. Kittredge looked at the dictionary phonetics with horror and drew a fountain pen from his pocket changing the phonetic signs so that they supported Kittredge's pronunciation. This only he properly could do since he was Editor-in-Chief of Webster's International Dictionary.

Professor Kittredge was deemed a monster for requiring as a condition for getting a grade better than "C" in English II ("Shakspere") the memorization of 500 lines on his theory that we should stuff good things into our minds. I thank him still as I pull out of the caverns of my memory appropriate verses or even whole speeches; "In such matters one must be his own physician," only those without memories seriously put down the cultivation of memory.

I learned about the romantic poets from James Livingston Lowes, a small man often seen in a salt and pepper tweed suit standing very erect. He spoke with a precise and beautifully enunciated Back Bay accent; this, semi-nasal sound as everyone knows, is, or was believed by most Americans, to be close to mother England. It was not until I had many contacts with Englishman that I realized that a Bostonian's speech is about as remote from Oxonian speech as it is from the speech of a Kentucky hillbilly. Lowes' course in the romantic poets was a revelation. He read lines of verse in the great acting tradition of John Barrymore and the

American Shakspere stage which combines declaiming with tremendous feeling and emphasis into a happy, if artificial mix. His love for the poets was real and his analysis of passages that needed analysis was stimulating and learned. I remember still his book called, "Convention and Revolt in Poetry," in which the opening paragraphs suggested that he was lying on a beach experiencing the physical sensations of light , color, line, sound, taste and smell and trying as a poet might to put these sensations into words. A few lines tell us the remarkable sensitivity and delicate use of words which Lowes sometimes was able to transmit to the student: "sound — the slow, recurrent, rhythmic thunder of the sea, the wind through the grass and in my ears, like Dante's voice within a voice; touch — the texture of the sand as I sift it through my fingers, the wind, soft and flowing across my body, the warmth of the sun felt beneath the wind; taste and smell — the fresh salty tang of the sea. And those are but a moiety of the sum." He taught us that words are but symbols and cannot be objects. Their meaning is only in relation to the unspeakable objects formed in the imagination where are found the energizers, and our word creations often live their own lives. Chesterton said of Dickens' Pickwick Club that Dickens came to scoff and stayed to pray.

One autumn day Lowes brought to the classroom a copy of a manuscript page from Keats' *Eve of St. Agnes.* He asked us to get our own copies which were made available at Widener, the college library, to demonstrate what so many seemed to have forgotten, that genius is the end product of hard work. Keats has, in the thirtieth stanza of that poem, a phrase describing the delicacies which her lover, Porphyro, brought to the fair Madeline: "With jellies soother than the creamy curd, and lucent syrops, tinct with cinnamon." Note the phrase "tinct with cinnamon."

The manuscript shows a margin in which perhaps twenty-five different words are used before Keats arrives at "tinct with cinnamon." They run around the page like a chain, one word stricken out, replaced by another, until it is apparent to all who care to know that this phrase did not fall off the poets lips like stretched bubble gum, but came as the product of the endless effort of a writer who set his standards so high that he must have searched for hours to find the final expression found in three words. On many occasions I have thought in the interest of time, particularly in the preparation of law briefs, to let something less than best go by either in my own or in the writing of others. I can hear the little man saying "tinct with cinnamon," pronouncing each syllable with precision, calling out to me to do better for, even if talent sometimes moves as a lightning bolt, its presence is not enough. As our parents have often said, genius includes the infinite capacity to take pains. Lowes was not ashamed of his propaganda for hard work, and indeed it seemed to be the objective of the English department to prevent itself from being identified with snap courses by piling on reading and requiring the writing of difficult examination essays.

There were others in the department whom I remember now with gratitude because of their interest in my writing. Bernard DeVoto was one; Robert Hillyer another. Some were flamboyant like my tutor, Rodney Bilkes. Some were dry as dust, like professor Robinson who edited the Cambridge Edition of "Chaucer," but they all pushed us on to a sense of the precision and flexibility of language and made us all "tinct" with the wonder of great prose and poetry. If nothing else came from this academic discipline, it was the life-long pleasure of reading Shakspere with the sense that the words were wonderful and friendly. Incidently, Robinson delayed the printing of "Chaucer" for forty years, thirty-six of them in the Twentieth Century, in order to have the advantage of the latest scholarship about a poet who lived in the Fourteenth Century and he would have preferred to have the book printed posthumously.

It is a Harvard tradition that many years ago in a dormitory in the Yard there lived a student named Reinhard. On pleasant spring evenings the Yard echoed with the calls of friends to friends and with the exchange of invitations and pleasantries among the students. But Reinhard's name was never called out because Reinhard had no friends. One evening the cry of "Reinhard" was heard loud and strong from under his window, repeated again and over again. It was not the voice of a friend calling to him, it was Reinhard himself who had raised the racket; Reinhard who stood in the shadow of his dormitory and cried out his own name. Even now Harvard students celebrate this tradition by opening their windows on spring evenings and calling out the name of this friendless student of bygone days.

There were many lonely nights when I was a student at Cambridge, Massachusetts—lonely not for lack of friends but lack of resolution of the anxieties that gnawed away at me, and from the sense of being alone, even with friends around me. It is not the existence of friends or even loving which ends lonliness, it is the sense of being one with others and not an outsider; lonliness is not being alone, but being lost in a universe of unfriendly objects and stars and planets that glower coldly from the sky.

The life of a man is, in large measure what he says about it. It holds love and fear, rage and contentment, understanding and ignorance, in continuous ferment as man tries with his limited tools to catch from the darkling sky a glimmer of what the human experience means.

I could only admire the austere, sexless statement of Walter Savage Landor, written at age ninety, "Nature I loved, and next to nature, art"; but I have found life to be an exquisite welter of emotional and rational experiences inextricably tied together and I cannot allow any real devotion to a concept so abstract as nature or so civilized as art.

For a large part of my life I upbraided myself because anxiety and other crippling emotional sets seemed to prevent me from living it fully. It took a long time to realize that the great struggles are not with the casual enemies who arise from the earth as shapeless blobs and disappear with a passage of time or a sweet kiss. It took a long time to realize that the real enemies who hold the hand from its proper work and dim the vision, often blinding it to a pinpoint of fear, are within. When these are conquered, life can become an exquisite exercise of mind and wit against the nasties of reality.

The tutorial system had just been introduced a year or two before my arrival in Cambridge. My tutor was a tall, frail man and regarded as remarkable for his memory and his ability to quote from the British poets. He went everywhere in a state of intoxication, carrying in his arms or leading by leash an equally alcoholic dachshund. He would come to visit his tutees escorted by a taxicab driver who parked his taxi at the nearest available spot and waited to be sure our tutor got safely back and forth to his digs. It was said that he started the day with martinis. I cannot vouch for this, but I know that he ended the day with martinis.

The purpose of the tutorial system was to augment the fields of concentration with correlated learning other than that being received from a formal course. My little tutorial group read Sophocles and Homer, mostly aloud, while the tutor sipped martinis and his dog lay semi-rigid on the rug. Kitteredge and others had much to say about the character of students; equal attention, however, was not given to faculty members. I, for one, viewed my tutor with increasing horror as it was made plain that his addiction was destroying the clarity of his intellect.

Sometimes when we came to impassioned scenes in Sophocles' Antigone, where Antigone defies Creon the King, our tutor would burst into tears much to the astonishment of the ten or twelve students who constituted the tutorial circle. Sometimes he would seize upon a word, play with it like a puppy with a tennis ball, saying it slowly, speeding it up, supplying information about its origins, and in effect making a verbal ballet of the writings of that ancient Greek. In my senior year he disappointed us all greatly by disappearing from the scene. We were told that he had gone to a British sanitarium to dry out and had experienced a nervous breakdown. We never saw him since nor, as far as I know, did Harvard. There are times when I pick up Homer and find the passage about the shield with its remarkable prediction of things to come, or dip into the plays of ancient Greece when even now my eyes moisten and my heart beats faster, racing with the excitement of the printed word, some of which was instilled in me by the frenzied enthusiasm of my drunken tutor.

The regulations for students in Harvard College in 1934 included these:

> Women shall not enter the Houses, dormitories, or club houses unattended; and a student, when entertaining women guests, should see that they are properly escorted.

> A student living in a house must obtain special permission from the Master or the Senior Tutor to receive women guests in his room .

> A student living in a University dormitory or elsewhere other than in a house must obtain special permission from the Proctor or the Regent to receive women guests in his room. Such permission will be granted only when a chaperon is to be present.

My recollection is that in the lobby leading to an entry in Kirkland House there was a sign which said, "No women or pets allowed in the room after 7:00 p.m." I trust my recollection is faulty, but there is no doubt that salty old graduates of Harvard College in recent years felt somewhat deprived when learning of coeducational dormitories and the permissive rules which permit young men and women to sleep together and otherwise make damn fools of themselves if they so desire. Indeed, I have been informed that in some university dormitories young men and women are lodged in the same entries. Since nature has a built in balancing gyroscope, a kind of incest taboo sets in so that the co-mingling of the sexes does not result in a continuing saturnalia. AIDS will probably set the mores back to the Elizabeth Barrett Browning period.

You are not to suppose that stern rules such as those requiring chaperons and women to leave the rooms by 7:00 p.m. were always followed, but the breaches of the rules had a kind of desperado flair with sentries posted on the lookout for proctors or faculty; elaborate arrangements were made for leaving houses at night, such as attempts at camouflage, when a young woman, wearing her swain's trenchcoat and sloppy hat made a quick exit off the premises. Parietal rules after all reflected the times in which they were written. They did not seem unduly repressive to most of us. But the sexual relations among college people were generally of such an order that it might be futile for a woman to stay overnight, especially if her young admirer was spending the time writing poetry in her honor—thus substituting verbal for physical caresses, and perhaps not quite certain of the difference.

The idea of virginity was still strong in the 1930s and the male libido seemed to be generally concentrated on the "townees" or non-college girls, who by force of misfortune of not going to the University were believed to have more submissive standards than others. The myths which grew up about the relations between the sexes were rarely tested in practice. It may well have been true that sexual experiences, when finding their way into conversations, were greatly exaggerated to the supposed benefit of the speaker. I knew a junior who claimed that he called up all of the single women in the phone book on the theory that one of the fifty would show some interest in him. I never believed this but thought it simply an application of the old joke about the college boy who continually walked around campus with a face battered and bruised and a black eye; and the explanation given was that he asked every pretty girl he met whether she would sleep with him. The justification for his doleful physical condition was this—they say "yes" every fiftieth time.

It was an age of big talk and little action in matters of sex. Marriage was taken more seriously than now and long engagements often took place when a young man felt that his income was inadequate to support his bride even though she herself might be gainfully employed. It was an age where marriage meant permanence and children. The divorce rate in the 1930s was less than twenty percent, as compared with sixty percent reached in some states today. It may be argued that this devotion to promises led to vast unhappiness as mismated couples clung together in an exercise of stamina and courage as well as masochism. It may with equal force be argued that love grew with kept promises.

The tuition fee for students in regular standing at Harvard College was, in 1931, $400 a year. The $400 was payable in four separate installments.

The price of rooms in the House varied from $100 to $600, depending on location and size. Each suite included a study, a bath and two bedrooms.

We ate in the common room of Kirkland House. I was introduced to such oddities as prune whip, hasty pudding and green beans which were served brown from over cooking.

We were charged $7.50 a week for meals, which entitled us to choose any ten meals in the course of a week offered by the House. If we took fourteen meals a week, the price was $8.50; and if all twenty-one meals were taken, the price was $10.50. Some weeks in which I took the $7.50 option, I made do with ten meals, augmenting them with crackers and milk.

Kirkland House accommodated about 200 students chosen in equal numbers from the three upper classes and selected so as to represent as nearly as possible a cross section of the College.

The master of the House was Edward Allen Whitney, whose lean Anglo-Saxon features sometimes could be seen at the dinner table. Other faculty members who were residents included what Charles Dickens was pleased to call "originals." There was Andre Morize, a professor of French Literature on loan from the University of Paris, and Arthur Colby Sprague, the learned roly-poly who served for a time as my advisor. Some twenty-five years later, he did the same service for my daughter, Jessica, when she was a student at St. John's of Annapolis, that curious college that believes in the emergence of civilization and the reading of what came to be known as "Great Books." I greatly admired the St. John's intellectual concept that the individual mind should repeat the learning growth process of all Western civilization.

I recall my daughter tussling with Ptolomaic demonstrations made in a false geometry, but one which had ruled the mind of Greece before Euclid. I remember her excitement in discovering in her junior year the circulation of the blood through the reading of essays by Thomas Harvey. She debated the important questions of good and evil, truth and falsity, through the study of Plato's Dialogues, and it seems to me that no better source of discussion of such matters has been developed since.

College life in the 1930s embraced a keen awareness of the Depression and a continuing dispute over what could be done about it. The economists of the 1930s were just as empty as the economists of the 1990s. They may have pretended a little more to knowledge of what was going on, but the violent solutions of technocrats, Stalinism and other extreme solutions to the fix we were in did not find wide support. Rather, Roosevelt, the tinkerer, the tacker, saved this nation at a time of its greatest uncertainty. Although he was a "New Deal" Democrat, one would expect to find him applauded by Bush and the Republican community because he saved the system. In saying this, the premise, of course, is made that the system was in trouble. Don't tell me otherwise, I was there.

I remember going to the basement of a Liggett's store, on the corner of 72nd and Broadway, in order to satisfy a demand of nature, and seeing, under the glare of a hanging light, among wooden crates and discarded cardboard boxes, a bed upon which an elderly man seemed to be coughing his life away, while next to him, on a simple stool, sat a woman, obviously his wife. If there were no rats around at that moment it was only because they were attending exercise class.

I remember seeing men standing in the Times Square subway next to little egg crates that had been given to them, and over the crates were little mounds of Delicious apples. Next to the boxes were signs such as, "I am a lawyer" and "I am a doctor." Don't say that I exaggerate. I saw this with my own eyes when I was an impressionable schoolboy, and the image has not gone away.

I remember seeing a line slowly moving from about 46th Street to the back of the New York

Times Building at 42nd Street and Broadway, where men and women were given bowls of soup, ladled out to them by volunteers.

This was America in 1932 and 1933 and, in the quiet luxury of our Harvard House, we often talked into the middle of the night presenting imperfectly thought-through solutions for the fix we were in. These were serious times. There were plenty of capers, but important to university life was the bull session, in which we did not hesitate to challenge the world. We did not, however, do it by carrying out deans from their offices, nor insisting upon control of academic progress. What we did was to challenge each other and often challenge the basis for our beliefs. Out of Harvard there rolled hundreds of young men from the law school, from the business school and from the college, who went to Washington determined to set the economy right without, perhaps, realizations of the limitations of government.

My college years also exposed me to a whole array of false values, many of which were the success values of that time. The suits uniformly came from Brooks, Finchley and DePinna. Of these, only Brooks still survives, and many Harvard men wear Brooks' clothes from early childhood to the grave as if they were a badge of social superiority. In my era when the Back Bay intonation was the standard for faculty and many of the students, one began to hear the same pseudo English accent from sturdy Georgians and prize high school scholars from Kansas City. White buck shoes were still in vogue, as was the brown or heather sports jacket with leather patches applied to the elbow points. Ties were worn to classes. Indeed, although nothing was said about it, ties seemed to be de rigueur both in the classroom and in the nearby restaurants, and almost everywhere.

It was not possible for even the Boston Brahmin to escape the common man. The common man was suffering, the newspapers told us so; the magazine articles described widespread poverty and the sense of revolt against the status quo which had seeped into the conscience of America. Amos and Andy said during the Depression that status quo is "Latin for the fix we're in." Most of the intellectuals and other students were radicals, but generally not Stalinists, nor believers in the seizure of the means of production, nor the dictatorship of the proletariat. Marx was much talked about, but rarely read. For sheer turgidity *Das Kapital* was rivaled only by Henry George's *Theory of the Leisure Class.* If the attitudes of my peers can be categorized at all simply, they were ,skeptical of solutions; but eager to find them; and they believed in the democratic dream fervently, thinking that Bryce was right when he said that it is to the people one must come sooner or later in every political matter. We believed in the people and the polls, and not the destruction of the status quo. But, we were uncommitted and saw no reason why the government could not tinker with economic institutions. There was a strong feeling that means of transportation such as railroads, ought to be government owned and that licensing of the airways for private use subjected the users to an overriding public obligation. We believed in experimentation professionally as well as politically, and at the same time in Washington the great tinkerers had sprung into power. REA brought electrification to outlying farmhouses which no private utility was prepared to service. NRA was a powerful effort to secure compliance of manufacturers, workers and others to a code set up in each industry with the purpose of assuring that industry could produce under circumstances protecting both laborer and the consumer. The Blue Eagle soared until it was shot down by a conservative U.S. Supreme Court intervening on the side of kosher butchers in Brooklyn.

Through subsidies, attempts were made to reinvigorate the bank accounts of despairing farmers and youths were kept off the streets by being offered useful employment through the Civilian Conservation Corps. The New Deal had many of its roots among Harvard academics who, upon graduation during the 1930s, hastened to Washington and were often able successfully to convert their abstract thinking into legislation. We were, however, imbued with concepts of the social contract, horror at star chamber proceedings, dictatorship, and curtailment of free speech; we identified with the "underdog", the little man, the citizen often being ground down by the "interests."

We often talked far into the night attempting to link what we knew as society's problems to our sources of wisdom who mostly had never heard of an automobile or a chain gang, but could, like Plato, define good and evil, and like Sir Francis Bacon, stress the triumph of truth over falsehood. We dealt with concepts far removed from the struggles at Weirton Steel or at the Dearborn bridge where company goons, employed by Ford, beat to death a number of union men. My group, whatever its pretense to pure intellectualism, may also have lived out the volatile emotions of the last few years of teenagery. I was almost always in love. I wrote poetry to my worshipped ladies, but shied away at the same time from the full sexual relationships which might have pushed me towards the disaster of marriage. I was amorous, but afraid, and I suppose, so were many of my contemporaries.

I was madly in love with a beautiful blonde young woman who was gloriously endowed with a sense of humor, and could herself, write poems to me and was very active in Wellesley. political affairs such as the Model League of Nations. One night I drove her to some young lady's home where she was to spend the weekend. I had rented a car, and this was for us a great adventure, since my funds were small, and the opportunity to travel by car was not often presented.

I was overwhelmed by the perfume and nearness of this wonderful lady. Finally, we reached the house where she would spend the next few days and where I could not enter with her—the hour being late and the home not her own. We passionately embraced on the porch, and she said to me, "This means we are engaged, doesn't it?" I returned to Cambridge in a state of trauma. Engagement was the farthest thing from my mind. Certainly my mother would not approve of a Mid-Western, Presbyterian girl, and certainly I would not be weighted down by the burden of an engagement. I stayed up most of that night writing her a long letter in which I explained that I was really a man of low character, that I drank too much, and that nothing but bad could come of a permanent relationship with me. Within forty-eight hours I received my reply. My loving girlfriend copied Shakspcrc's 116th Sonnet:

> "Let me not to the marriage of true minds
> admit impediments: Love is not love
> which alters when it alteration finds."

Now, I truly ran frightened. My fair one loved me enough to countenance me even if I were Jack the Ripper. This was too much for a Harvard sophomore. I decided to ignore her letters, but had the stamina only to do this once and then remorse, reconciliation. The sophomore year began to drag me out of adolescence. She went back for the summer to Illinois and I to White Plains, New York; and one hot August morning I received a letter which told me that she had met the man of her dreams, that he lived out her way, and that they were going to be married. One part of me rejoiced that I had dropped the albatross; the other did not, and in that stirring cauldron which is human memory, even as I dictate this manuscript, there remains a tinge of the pain of loss and a sense of joy that as a sophomore I could experience romantic love, and that I had continued to experience it throughout a long life.

Other young ladies in that almost forgotten time came in and out of my life without my fully appreciating that they were young human beings like myself; eager to learn a little about living, frightened, uncertain, and not yet ready to face up to such weighty matters as the perpetuation of the human race, the matter of working in the competitive society, and the home away from home that had nurtured them.

Sex was sought after in rather desultory fashion, and casual experiences were often most unsatisfactory, accompanied by whiskey to brace up courage and with little recognition of the needs and desires of the girls participating in such casual episodes. A sister of a friend of mine was a Radcliffe student. She had rather coarse, but attractive features. She seemed to me to be very much a woman of the world. I remember that she was very blonde, her figure full, and her lips were large. She walked in a most sensuous manner, at least as I perceived her. We had a very casual romance which culminated as follows. It was near examination time and my lady had the need to submit a term paper in some field where I had taken no course and possessed no particular knowledge—I think it was sociology. She invited me to her room on a Sunday afternoon, and since she did not live in a dormitory, we were not subject to the usual restrictions imposed against the mating of the sexes. She had on her desk three or four textbooks relating to the subject matter; and I was not there long when she explained to me that she was totally unable to write her term paper, that, if I did not do it for her, she doubtless would flunk out of Radcliffe; and if I did it for her I would receive all of the favors which this luxurious young woman could afford. I proceeded to read the first paragraph or two in each chapter of her books and made careful notes concerning the chapter headings and whatever I supposed was the ground structure of the course. This took me well into the night, at which time I dictated while she typed directly on her typewriter her term paper in this alien field. I completed it with a sense of triumph about 3:00 or 4:00 in the morning, and as I fell asleep I heard her typing over the paper for submission in class that very morning. I fell soundly asleep and awakened towards dusk, noticing that my roommate was not present and my rewards not available; and I had been absent from two classes of my own. I then returned to my room a somewhat wiser young man, able to observe for the first time that not all women are goddesses. My recollection is that I never saw the young woman again but she called me to say gratefully that she had gotten a "B minus" on her paper.

I studied and debated for Harvard, talked incessantly, played some chess, listened to music, worried a lot and began to be suffused with guilt as it became clear to me near the end of my undergraduate stay that my mother was losing her grip on reality, that the distress of her living alone and her inability to succeed in her little real estate business during the depth of the Depression, were too much for her. As the banks took her property away by foreclosing mortgages, they also took the firm and courageous mien which she generally displayed. Her voice, which to me had always seemed like a quiet aria, speaking in sentences full of metaphors, similes and poetic references, began to take on a desperate fibre. During my last college year it became apparent that she was showing the symptoms of incipient paranoia. She then lived in a rented apartment in a two-family house and professed she could hear the couple above threatening her with dire violence. I did nothing to relieve her loneliness, but a sense of guilt concerning her had begun to seep into my consciousness.

As a debater, I enjoyed great success. We debated against Stanford in a transcontinental radio hookup. The subject was "Resolved that College Education is Worthwhile." Harvard took the negative. Some days later, I received a postal card from a young woman in Brooklyn, New York, thanking me for giving her the arguments to use against her parents who wanted her to go to College. I frantically responded that she must never believe debaters; although we had argued that a college education was not worth while, it really was worthwhile and she better heed the advice of her parents. This was one of the many dramas in which I've participated without ever finding out what happened in the last act.

We went on a debating trip to the hills of Pennsylvania, where we debated Haverford, Franklin and Marshall, and Villanova on the Vinson Navy Bill which in 1933 called for the rebuilding of our navy that had been scuttled by force of the Locarno Pact of the 1920's following the First World War. We took both sides at different colleges, and at Villanova my teammate, Seymour Peyser, had difficulty in putting on his tuxedo. This tuxedo was the very same one he had purchased during his senior year at high school for The New York Times Oratorical contest concerning the Constitution of the United States. I had also survived to the finals (won by Peyser) and at about the same time had acquired my tuxedo. In dressing for the debate it became apparent to Peyser that he needed no belt nor suspenders to keep his trousers up. He amply filled his tuxedo. At the debate the speaker from Villanova immediately preceding Peyser made the rafters ring with his statement that, "The gentlemen from Harvard are optimists and I define an optimist as a person who wears neither suspenders nor a belt." Opportunity is not always so kind to Harvard men. Peyser was kicked by both his teammates at the same time but needed no prodding from us. He rose from the table majestically and said, "Ladies and Gentlemen, the gentleman from Villanova is quite right. We are optimists"— and at this he opened his jacket and vest—"as you can see, my trousers stay up very well indeed." This powerful argument brought stupendous applause and doubtless was the principal reason for our winning the debate. It is probable that important matters such as the size of our navy cannot in real life be decided on grounds so substantial as this.

We debated Princeton and Yale in the Annual Triangular Debate on the subject "Resolved that a National Police Force Should be Created." My team had the negative. More than a half century has gone by and there has been no federal police force. That apparently was our most successful college debating victory. One year I served as Chairman for the delegates for Siam (now Thailand) to the Model

League of Nations (prior to the existence of the United Nations). A disproportionate number of students from Harvard represented that tiny kingdom. At an appropriate moment I rose and challenged the great powers to disarm, offering to set an example by disarming right away and disarming our navy first. We had read somewhere that Siam operated two or three junks on the China Sea equipped with light weapons, but it wasn't very important whether or not Siam had a Navy, we were prepared to junk it. When the general assembly, dominated by the great powers, showed no willingness to join in a disarmament program, we dramatized our position by walking out of the meeting. In doing so we may have set a dangerous precedent for our elders who frequently behaved like that after the United Nations was formed. We did learn through our maneuver a little bit of politics, since the unexpected and dramatic exit made all the papers and tended to give the impression, which in fact was true in 1933, that college students wanted peace and equated peace with disarmament.

Thus I was graduated magna cum laude and eligible to address the commencement exercise if I could win in competition involving my peers. I triumphed over my adversaries who doubtless were better scholars and found myself designated to represent the class of 1934 in the English dissertation given at the commencement exercises. These exercises were faithfully attended by faculty, graduates and their families. and various dignitaries from the political and scholarly world.

My mother had arrived for the ceremony. She was in my room when Professor Maynadier entered—the evening before commencement. Maynadier was an extremely courteous New Englander, white crew-headed, and for a time my mother and he hit it off swimmingly. Her face was animated, her clothes, although somewhat ancient, were trim and stylish in the manner of the times. She was proud of me and the conversation was happy in tone. Shortly before the Professor was about to take his leave, she asked sweetly, "Do you know about the Gargins?" The grizzly headed professor confessed he did not. "The Gargins are going to kill me, you know," she matter-of-factly stated. The professor looked at me with a deep expression of empathy and compassion. "When I return to White Plains," she added. The professor hastened his departure, and my mother and I stared at each other across a canyon of misunderstanding, pain, and ignorance which never could be crossed. My remarks at commencement were devoted to books. I was far too young to understand the meaning of agony.

I soon took my mother to her hotel room, which she shared with one of her sisters. It was, as far as I can remember, her one and only trip to Cambridge, Massachusetts. She sat through the ceremonies the next day. I watched her and she seemed proud. I heard no other references to her obsession, and those who met her that day thought her a bright and interesting lady. The boon I have asked of and have been denied by Zeus is that we only suffer today for the pain of the day, rather than the pain of years. We all went back home in a day or two to pick up a different life, of a kind of darkening tension with a tight feeling in the air and the heart and the conviction that soon a storm would come.

I would make a speech about books. I said nothing of Mercer's collection of books, which could not be read because the illustrations were too fine. Perhaps the last words on learning from books were not mine but the Country Squire's, which is to be found in that splendid collection that delighted my youth, *Journeys Through Bookland.* The Country Squire, who was a man of greater wealth than wit, built a new house and commissioned the building of a library.

But ere the library was half supplied
With all its pomps of cabinet and shelf,
The booby squire repented him, and cried
Unto himself:

Now, as I only want them for their looks,
It might, on second thoughts, be just as good
And cost me next to nothing, if the books
Were made of wood.

The work was done, the simulated boards
Of wit and wisdom round the chamber stood,
In binding some;and some, of course, in boards
Where all were wood.

What wonder, as he paced from shelf to shelf
And conned their titles, that the squire
began,
Despite his ignorance, to think himself
A learned man?

The morning of June 3, 1934 was grey and threatening, but the rain held back. We lined up early in cap and gown. Because of my sudden elevation of function, I stood at the head of the student line of graduates in the Yard, and we separated into two facing lines to let the dignitaries march through. These were many, and included Senators, the Governor, a Rear Admiral, Chief of Staff for the Headquarters of the First Corp area, Mayor Russel of Cambridge, Mayor Mansfield of Boston, President Emeritus A. Lawrence Lowell, and many others who filled black robes with dignity. According to *The Boston Globe*, President Conant conferred the degrees "by virtue of the authority vested in him." The reporting went on:

The Commencement parts, always a feature of Commencement Day, are delivered by honor candidates for degrees in the University.

This year, the traditional Latin greeting, was given by Paul L. MacKendrick, '34. of Roslindale. Two "parts" were given in English, one by Malcolm A. Hoffmann, '34, White Plains, New York, and the other by Reginald G. Buehler, A.B. Yale, '19, A.M. Harvard, '20.

MacKendrick's Latin greeting began with the customary "Salvete Omnes" and included a reference to "puellae formosissimae ac venustissimae" which brought smiles to the faces of the ladies present who happened to know Latin.

Hoffmann's address, entitled "Of the Critical Faculty," was the next of the program. The tall senior from White Plains whose work has been a strong point in Harvard debating of the last three years, spoke of the "ability to make personal judgements which will most closely accord with all the relevant data."

He spoke of college years as years of acquiring wisdom without experience of real life, yet maintained that the learning gained from books made a person more critical of life and better able to meet its problems.

Hoffmann said:

"For four years this senior class has lived more or less intensively in a world of books. Life for the educated man is of two worlds—the world of actuality, which many of us are facing for the first time, which some of us will never face, and the world of books, which is reflected actuality, and of our acquaintance since first we learned to read. There are many differences which divide these worlds as if by sharp and indestructible cleavers...Divorced from the pressures of the world of actuality, we have nevertheless endeavored to comprehend wisdom born of the pressure of actuality. The function of the books and the academic life of the past four years is to teach us the lesson in advance of the experience. The experience will come, perhaps even before we have mastered the lesson. But, when it comes these books will acquire a new significance. Those which are of value will prove real, as the pain of life is real. Life will have made us critical of books, and books have made us critical of life."

Next night I took the "red-eye" from Back Bay Station, Boston, to New York City. I found my mother in her White Plains apartment. She held me frantically, looking in my eyes for the help I could not give her.

Aaron Holtzman

(1927-1965)

Aaron Holtzman was my friend. Often he stood with his palms turned outward in conversation, as if appealing for attention. He stood 5 feet 4 or 5 inches tall, and he spoke clearly and with great deliberation. Aaron had been valedictorian of his class at White Plains High School, in a class two years ahead of mine. He lived in White Plains not far from me. From the period when we were in high school until his untimely death in 1965, we remained fast friends, and now I must write something of this remarkable man.

Aaron, whom we often called "A" for short, read omnivorously. He relied upon an extraordinary memory; often he preferred to use his precise recollection of the printed page to his own original thought. Aaron had received all A's in three universities over a four-year period and was not elected to Phi Beta Kappa, nor did he receive a Bachelor's

Degree. This honors contretemps came about as follows:

He started at New York University's University Heights College for a year, transferred to Cornell, and then having decided upon a career in journalism, returned from Ithaca to New York City and on to the Columbia School of Journalism, which at that time required 3 years in residency for a degree. In his fourth college year, in 1933, when his father's manufacturing business collapsed, one morning, instead of taking the train to New York, his father gathered his flock together and made the statement that they could obtain no more money from the bank, that he had paid all his debts, except for mortgages, and had assets of $29 even. The situation was the more poignant because Aaron's father, like many immigrants from Central Europe, greatly loved this country, and during his affluent days, which lasted until the depths of the depression, he showed himself to be the most generous of men. He owned a tall Seventh Avenue building in the dress district of New York City, where often he excused rents from his tenants when times were bad. He had an entire floor for his own manufacturing company, but when the banks repossessed the building under a defaulted mortgage, he promptly was evicted. He once gave a shoeshine boy who used to treat his shoes at the White Plains railroad station a thousand dollars to go to college because he was convinced that the boy was intelligent. When something moved him, his impetuous generosity had no limits, reaching celestial height when he purchased the Bedford Hills Country Club — a rich man's golf club, equipped with large buildings and golf course — with the object of creating a comfortable rest home for people in the garment industry.

I remember this little man well, always poorly shaved and with a cigar butt in his mouth. When all others had left him, he went to work in a small space with one helper — still a proud manufacturer and still confident that great and generous America the beautiful would enable him to make a fortune once more. On that fateful day in 1933 when old Jake Holtzman came home and surrounded himself with his children, it was decided that Aaron would leave the halls of learning and attempt to make a living.

"A" got a job in an advertising office as a copywriter for a small salary, and never was there a man more unsuited for his profession. He wrote clearly and well, but the truth was an obsession for him and conniving was not in him. He believed that the purpose of an advertisement was to tell the customer faithfully the quality and the price of the merchandise being offered. Incidentally, the ad might also say where the merchandise could be obtained; beyond that he would tolerate no puffing or cutting corners. He became very much respected by his advertising peers, probably because he was such a phenomenon. After working for someone else, he formed a little agency of his own which provided what in those days was known as "a living." Ultimately, Aaron was married and lived the life of the intelligent New York City middle class.

Aaron came to be my guest at the Harvard Law School within a few days after I started that difficult regime in 1934, because I held the idea that we ought to put in dramatic form the short stories of Poe and, I thought we could work better in collaboration if he were in Cambridge with me. So he became a guest on a cot in my room for a period of about a month, in the course of which, we adapted four or five Poe stories and sold them all to the Yankee Network for a total of $90; a vast sum of money in our opinion, but a little miserly for so many radio scripts. We ultimately heard one or two acted on the network. I remember the late-at-night writing sessions, which might better have been spent on contracts and torts, when we snarled at each other, reading aloud from Poe's *Cask of the Amontillado,* accepting Poe's marvelous dialogue and supplementing it with some of our own. I remember well the lines from the original. "Luchesi is a fool. He cannot distinguish Amontillado from Sherry." Much later I discovered that Poe was pompously wrong. Amontillado is nothing more than a dark, strong, rich sherry.

When he had returned to New York, and I to my law studies, I had not yet abandoned the thought of writing for a career. The summer before law school began, we had together determined that we should be Hollywood script writers. We wrote a letter to a person who was known as an imaginative and impetuous impressario in Hollywood named Irving Thalberg. Our letter in effect described ourselves as extraordinarily talented, appealed to the ability of Thalberg to recognize true genius, and suggested that we would be prepared to help his enterprises with our writing skills. We did not, however submit a manuscript along with our application. Some weeks later, near the end of the summer, we received a telephone call from someone in Manhattan, perhaps named Sam Blank, but of his name I can no longer be sure. He said in effect, "Come to see me at such and such a room at the Hotel Astor, I am Mr Thalberg's agent." We hailed a stunning triumph. We saw Blank as soon as he would receive us. Once again, we made a remarkable presentation of glistering words and sterling representations about our writing skills. Mr. Blank was somewhat surprised and distressed that we had not brought a manuscript with us. He said, "Thalberg liked your letter. He instructed me to hire you if the movie script that you brought for me was any good. Do you have one at home?" We had none. We had not taken the precaution of writing a single movie script, nor even an outline;

we rather thought that was something one could only do in Hollywood, after, but not before, employment as a script writer. We suggested, however, that we would quickly prepare a script, and he said he would be back to New York in about two months and that we should see him again. Two months later I was ensconced in Cambridge at the Harvard Law School and my friend "A" was doing freelance writing in New York preliminary to the advertising career which shortly came upon him. "A" would go to the New York Public Library, study the Index to Periodicals and then write an article on subjects rarely found in the Index. I remember he was once paid (circa 1935) 40 dollars for an article on "Barber Poles".

I remember a Saturday night in Cambridge when "A" and I had too much to drink. We went to Boston with some classmates of mine and we walked on Boylston Street in a state of drunken euphoria. "A" suddenly made the sound of a horse whinnying. We stopped amazed. It seemed to us a faithful sound. "Whinny like a horse again, A", we coaxed him. And whinny he did for four or five blocks in the most sedate part of Boston, loudly and clearly and truly, he was a mite more of a horse than little Eohippus.

Aaron had one side of his face, which might have been extremely handsome, blighted by ascepsis, a very sizeable birthmark which ran up to the side of his scalp and interfered with hair growth above his right ear. He always seemed a little self-conscious about this flaw but he rarely spoke of it. He did seem timid in his dealings with women and he did not get married until close to age 40.

During the period of his 20's and 30's, it is not to be supposed that Aaron maintained a pad, played FM music and entertained the ladies. This was the repressed social period of the century. He put egg shells in his coffee and liked to cook poached eggs to which he added a spot of vinegar, "To hold them together." He was, under normal circumstances, quietly restrained in everything he did.

I was early married and Ann, "A" and I talked together, almost at university long distance lengths. We shared the most profound of our thoughts. We went over the news in constant conversation. We shared our reading. "A" and I liked to talk, not only to hear the sound of our own voices, but we learned to listen to others. In some imperfect way, we sought to grapple with the problems of the times. We even thought the mind was a muscle that needed constant exercising, and we played a great deal of chess and solved many puzzles. When there was trouble at hand, there was always "A" looking on the scene as if he were some kind of friendly angel. He was small in stature, but exuded support and affection. I in turn admired him, but his memory was so prominent and so strong that it was also a source of real annoyance. We might, in 1955, be discussing a matter, and Aaron would say "There was an article about this in Harper's for

March 1932. You remember Professor DeVoto said..." and then in what almost seemed to be a precise quote, he would squint his eyes and would bring to bear the learning of Professor DeVoto; not always quite relevant to the problem we had discussed, but relevatory of "A's" magnificent memory. More common would be a reference something like this; "How do you explain your position, "Mal" or "Hof", as he often called me, "When you were a college freshman, you said so and so and so." I could not deny that I had said, so and so and so. Nor could I affirm that: I had said so and so and so. Aaron had the most extraordinary memory that I'd ever encountered, and I've encountered some mighty ones, including Felix Frankfurter's. His memory was loaded with poetry not of the classical kind. He would, on the slightest pretext, recite from beginning to end, "Dangerous Dan McGrew" or even "Sam McGee" by the mighty poet, Robert Service. He was an afficionado of "Casey at the Bat". I, myself, learned much of his repertory, because he was not above repeating it again and again, particularly under convivial circumstances. "There are strange things done in the midnight sun by the men who moil for gold. The Arctic trails have their secret tales that would make your blood run cold. The Northern Lights have seen queer sights but the queerest they ever did see, was the night on the marge of Lake LeBarge, I cremated Sam McGee." And so it went on and on. He could sing no better than I, and we were mum when singing was in order, as often it was in the parties of our youth. But we could both quote poetry *ad tedium*, and this was a skill often called upon.

"A" was unlike shorter men, who frequently seem either obnoxiously aggressive, without a proper social check and seemingly desirous of cutting tall men down with scythes at the ankles. He was a gentle, humble man. But generalizations, of course, of this kind, if not amusing, ought not be made.

St. John's, that little college in Annapolis, Maryland, brought my daughter, Jessica, and William Davis together. They married and lived in an apartment on a hill in that city of many hills, Worcester, Massachusetts. One day Ann and I, and Aaron and his wife, Sue, drove to Worcester, where we held reservations at a new Holiday Inn, in order to spend the evening with the Davises and their parents at a little party that my daughter and her husband were offering. We drove from New York city in my car, and stopped for refreshment along the side of Conn. 15, when Aaron said to me, "I do not feel very well." He then said that he had been to his physician the day before, who had gone over him very carefully and told him that he was perfectly healthy. I asked him if he wanted to turn back and "A" said, "No", certain he would feel better later. Aaron was as good as his word. After we registered in the hotel, we made our way to my children's house, where "A" played an important role in the festivities. About midnight we returned to our rooms.

At 5:00 A.M., my wife and I were awakened by the knock of Susan, Aaron's wife, at the door. She announced, "A is dead". He'd awakened about 3:00 not feeling well; they attempted to get a doctor through the hotel's desk, but were told to drive instead to a nearby Worcester hospital. There, "A" sat in a chair waiting for an intern to come to take his history, and while time went by, perhaps a half-hour, he suddenly fell off his chair, and could not be revived The undertaker, with a cackling young New England patois, had called me with apparent pleasure, describing my friend, and observing that he was now lying naked on a marble slab. Arrangements were made for Aaron to be dressed and transported to New York.

We flew back with Sue, leaving our car in care of our children. Aaron apparently died from a heart attack. Once again, the blood of the dead was on my hands. If only we had not taken him to Worcester. If only I had insisted on turning back when Aaron complained, perhaps he would still be alive. Much of the human spirit is in constant disorder; we think we can pull ourselves out from ourselves and assume that we have command, or can influence the mighty course of events. We refuse to recognize ourselves as people inadequate, hardly able to take care of our own simplest needs, almost always unable to help others. Consciousness is a behavioral event, and there isn't a lot we can do about its contents.

As I was dictating this tale a moment ago, a heavily wetted piece of kitchen paper toweling, which was lying flat on an ashtray, unexpectedly popped over the edge and onto the floor; its movement did not seem to be explicable in terms of anything happening in the external world, in consideration of the force of gravity, that could be seen to be causative. Some might suspect the presence of a spirit; some might suspect some unknown psychokinetic force. The thought that Aaron was somewhere in the room trying to make himself known struck me for just a fraction of a point of time. The mind is so full of ghosts, of ancient pain, and of ancient longing, that it is not surprising if once in a while a little of it is not contained. A little of it forces its way out, and we are, once again, in the jungle howling out loud with the banshees, crying for fear, or joy, and facing always the opaque. The unknown link of space between us and our unknown enemies .

He lies naked, outstretched on the undertaker's table. The howl of the whistle of the night freight is not far away. His hands seem to have reached their accustomed posture; palms held up and open, as if supplicating nature. "I have come this far," says "A". "Why am I stopped now?" In this little back alley of civilization, this undertaker's motel for the dead, is my friend. Were there unknown tendrils of communication, private radio channels on which we had receivers, we would communicate with each other. His short life was more painful than most. It seemed to me that if nature were compassionate, he would have died grandly - not falling off a chair, waiting for help, in the last dark of night, in a heartless hospital in an unfriendly town.

Abby Gross

(1948-1958)

On a summer Saturday or Sunday afternoon during the 1950's, I often played chess with Abby Gross. Abby was no ordinary man, he was an honorable and four-square man. He wore light green heather suits, with leather patches at the elbows, big tortoise shell glasses. He had sandy hair and a "brrr" which rolled out like bowling balls. Abby was a graduate of the University of Edinburgh, a Scotchman, son of Scottish parents and grandparents. His occupation was to translate Yiddish novels into English. He performed this function surpassingly well, with Sholom Aleicheim, Sholom Asch, Peretz, and others, who were great figures in modern Yiddish literature. We generally called Abby "Pete" for reasons which were obscure then and unknown now.

He was a stocky man, perhaps 5' 10" or 6'. He smoked a pipe which was probably not a genuine meerschaum, but, nevertheless, showed aging and discoloration against the white bowl. I remember the tobacco sweetened the summer outdoors. It was a mixture of latakia and honey in a brand popular in that era. I sometimes am bewitched by the Irish and Welsh, but he told his stories in strong Scotch fiber in a kind of inflection which suggested you better listen to him.

His stories were based upon peasant life in small towns in Europe which more than two centuries ago were occupied by Jews. It was the Shtetl of Poland, and countless strange places immortalized by Shalom Aleichem and Peretz, more lately by Isaac Singer and Irving Howe in WORLD OF OUR FATHERS. He told the stories as we played our chess, and every once in a while, when it was necessary to think hard, he would interrupt the stories. Chess has its own song, a little refrain which goes, "If I go there, he goes there." "If I go there, he goes there." "If I go there, he goes there." That really is what the whole game of chess is about. The ability to project such calculations for some moves ahead.

But the stories Abby told, I have not heard elsewhere. They charmed me, and I have been able to please my friends by repeating this one.

Malcolm A. Hoffmann, Special Assistant to the Attorney General of the United States, in charge of antitrust prosecutions against IBM, RCA, General Electric, Swiss Watch Cartel and other cases. c.1950.

Malcolm A. Hoffmann to the left, David,his brother, to the right and Gertrude,
his sister, on the lap of his mother, Minna Hoffmann in New York City in 1916.

(2)   (Refer to Page 14)

MAH at age three, holding
a fishing pole at a farm
in Liberty, New York.

(3)   (Refer to Page 20)

MAH, age four, vacationing
at farm in New York with pail
in his hand.

(4)   (Refer to Page 22)

MAH's uncle, Isaac Newton Hoffmann,
Assistant Financial Editor of the
New York Times, writer and
consultant to financial journals.

(5)   (Refer to Page 27)

MAH's uncle, Jack Hoffmann,
a manufacturer of metal products
who lived most of his adult life in
Highland Park, Illinois. c.1945.

(6)   (Refer to Page 27, 28)

MAH's aunt, Therese Hoffmann, an artist and interior designer.

(7)   (Refer to Page 28)

MAH's father, Abraham Albert Hoffmann, reading in the garden of his home in New York City about 1898 at age 16.

(8)   *(Refer to Page 29)*

Father, Abraham Albert Hoffmann, mother, Minna Newmark,
and brother, David. c.1911.

(9) (Refer to Page 29)

MAH's mother, Minna Newmark, in 1900, before her marriage to
Abraham Albert Hoffmann.

(10)   (Refer to Page 41)

From left to right,
back row:
MAH's maternal aunts,
Miriam and Hattie,
father, Abraham
Albert Hoffmann,
mother, Minna
Hoffmann;
seated in front are
his maternal grand-
parents: grandmother,
Cecelia Newmark,
and grandfather,
Marcus B. Newmark,
holding brother David.
c.1910.

(11)
(Refer to Page 41)

Malcolm A. Hoffmann as a Senior at
White Plains High School in 1930.

(12)   *(Refer to Page 84)*

The pride, self-reliance
and compassion of
MAH's late wife, Anna
Frances Hoffmann, at
the height of her career
as the Director of the
Hoffmann School.

(13)   (Refer to Page 97)

Rebecca Hoffmann,
aunt of MAH and founder
of The Hoffmann School
in 1921. c.1945.

(14)   (Refer to Page 98)

MAH and wife, Anna,
in driveway of New York
home in 1950.

(15)   (Refer to Page 95)

Anna F. Hoffmann and
MAH at Riverdale home
after about 20 years
of marriage in 1959.

(16)   (Refer to Page 96)

MAH and Anna (his wife) and their daughter, Trudy, age two in 1942.

(17)   (Refer to Page 97)

MAH returns to
Harvard's Kirkland
House in 1986.
He lived there from
1931 to 1934.

(18)
(Refer to Page 111)

In August 1992, Harvard College Classmates of 1934 at Lowell's 80th birthday.
Reading from left to right, Carl Henry, C. Lowell Harriss, Clifford Rich and MAH.

(19)   (Refer to Page 146)

Hon. Christopher Symons, now Queen's Counsel. A barrister who worked
in MAH's office.

(20)   (Refer to Page 204)

Lord Elwyn Jones in full regalia as Lord Chancellor.

(21)   *(Refer to Page 207)*

Lord Jones at a party at MAH's home in August, 1974.

(22)   (Refer to Page 213)

Malcolm A. Hoffmann and the late Morris L. Ernst, co-authors of *Back and Forth*.

(23)   (Refer to Page 210)

Elwyn Jones and wife, Polly Binder campaigning for Parliament in 1945. et. seq.

(24)   (Refer to Page 207)

Lord Arnold Goodman, Baron of Westminster.

(25)   (Refer to Page 249)

MAH and Lord Goodman stalled on the Brighton Road
outside of London in 1966.

(26)   (Refer to Page 259)

Sir Robin Auld and MAH, 1983.

(27)   (Refer to Page 277)

Sir Robin Auld elevated to High Court, with his wife, Mary in 1988.

(28)   (Refer to Page 278)

MAH on the terrace of Riverdale, New York home in 1978.

MAH's daughter, Dr. Gertrude Bolter ("Trudy"), is an Associate Professor
at the University of Bordeaux in France where she received her Ph.D.
Her other degrees are from Bryn Mawr and Columbia University. She was
a Fulbright Fellow in Paris. Prior to entering academia, she was a staff writer
for *HARPERS BAZAAR* in New York. September, 1992.

Dr. Jessica Davis ("Jesse"), MAH's daughter, is a Research Associate and
Lecturer on Education at the Harvard Graduate School of Education.   She is
an author of numerous articles in the fields of psychology, eduction and art.
She holds a Bachelors Degree from Simmons College and Masters and
Doctoral Degrees from Harvard.

MAH's daughter, Trudy, with son-in-law, William Bolter, in July 1992.
Mr. Bolter is a graduate of the University of Edinburgh and is an owner of a
Bordeaux vineyard. He is the author of numerous articles about wines and
two books, *The White Wines of Bordeaux* and *The Red Wines of Bordeaux*.
The Bolters and their two daughters all live together in Bordeaux.

MAH's daughter, Jessica, with husband William Davis. He is a Senior Vice-President at Donaldson, Luftkin & Jenrette and Chairman of the Board of the Berklee College of Music. Mr Davis has a B.A. Degree from St. John's College in Annapolis, Maryland.

MAH and daughter, Trudy, in June 1991 in Ardsley, New York.

Miriam T. Miller ("Mimi"), retired Rutgers Law School Assistant Dean and loving friend of MAH holds a B.A. Degree from Wellesley and a J.D. from Rutgers Law School Newark.

Mimi in 1985.

In 1947. Trudy on the left and Jessica on the right, standing on the wide running
board of a 1933 Buick, purchased at the end of World War II when no cars were
available since the war had preempted the manufacturing of automobiles.
All used cars were said to be sold by older women who used them solely
to go back and forth to church on Sunday mornings.

First cousins: Jewel Miller on the right and Leonore Etler on the left in their
Tulsa, Oklahoma home at or about 1980.

Judge Millard Midonick and MAH's grandson, Joshua Davis, at Ardsley,
New York soon after the judge had presided over the marriage of Joshua
and Susan Flink in 1991.

The family, circa 1952, on Hoffmann School grounds, from left to right, MAH, AFH, Jessica Hoffmann holding Bruce II and Trudy Hoffmann.

It seems that in the Thirteenth Century in Prague, there was a pernicious anti-semitic feeling, since the people had forgotten that Jesus was a Jew, and many laws were promulgated, designed to harass the poor Jews. These laws culminated in an infamous edict issued by the Bishop of Prague, who was the chief religious leader of the community. The edict read "Unless a representative of the Jews shall defeat me, the learned Bishop of Prague, in debate, the head of the representatives will be forfeit, and the Jews immediately will be banished into exile." When the terms of this fell edict reached the Jewish Quarter of Prague, the Rabbi gathered his flock together and said he would debate the learned Bishop because, without question he was the most learned man amongst the Jews. A powerful man named "Yankel" mighty of arm, but somewhat feeble of intellect, rose and said, "Oh Rabbi, you must stay with us in our days of exile, which surely lie ahead, I shall go and debate the learned Bishop because even I am sure it makes no difference who debates him, the head of the Jew will be forfeit." And all applauded the courage of the young Yankel, a locksmith by trade.

It was thus that he confronted the learned Bishop in his chambers. The Bishop had also provided, that he, the Bishop of Prague, would be the sole arbiter of the merits of the debate. Yankel entered the Bishop's pretentious chambers. They were closeted together there for 10 or 15 minutes, and then Yankel returned to the Jewish Quarter of Prague, whilst the Bishop went out on his balcony and informed the elders of Prague that the ignorant Jewish locksmith had defeated him in debate. "How is it possible?" some of the elders asked. The Bishop replied, "As soon as he came in my room, I saw he was an ignorant man, and therefore he could not debate with me in Latin, which is the language of learned men, nor in Hebrew, which is the sacred language of his people. I could not debate with him in Yiddish, which is a language favored by the lesser element of the Jewish Community. Nor could I debate with him in Bohemian, which is the common language of the people of Prague, so I decided I must debate with him on some fair basis for communication, and that could only be signs. Consequently, I raised my whole hand, showing him that the Jews through their failure to accept Christ as the Savior, had been scattered across the face of the globe. And, as I raised my hand, he raised one finger at me, showing me that the Jews, although scattered through the Diaspora across the face of the globe, nonetheless through their stubborn belief in one God, remained united and strong. Thereupon, I raised three fingers to him, demonstrating that the failure of the Jews to accept the concept of the Holy Trinity, made them forever damned, and unable to go to heaven. In response to this, the young Hebrew raised his fist and shook it violently in front of me, indicating to me that the Jews, through their powerful belief in one God, would enjoy paradise. Finally, I pulled from the drawer of my desk, a bottle of good claret indicating to the Jew that the failure to accept the Holy Trinity and the coming of the Messiah and the Resurrection made their sins remain as red as that red wine. The young locksmith had an answer. He pulled from his jacket a piece of white cheese and showed it to me, proudly indicating to me that because of the stubborn and tenacious belief of the Jews in a single God, their sins were as white as that cheese. Thus it was that Yankel, the locksmith defeated me in debate, and so I have lifted the terms of the decree against the Jews."

When word of this triumph reached the Jewish sector, there was great joy, and Yankel was asked to explain how it was he was able to defeat the learned Bishop of Prague in debate. Yankel said, "I came into the Bishop's quarters, and there was this skinny old man, very angry, and he raised his whole hand as if to slap me. I raised a single finger to the Bishop, indicating that if he came a step closer, I could break his back with one finger only. The Bishop grew more angry and raised three fingers at me. I raised my fist at him, indicating to him that if he came an inch closer, I would knock his head off. The Bishop saw how things were going and decided to make friends with me. He brought out a bottle of red wine. Now all I had with me to share was a piece of white cheese that Becky gave to me in case I got hungry."

Pete Gross was proof of the international quality of civilized man. His ethnic origins included native Scotch Presbyterians, a strain of Jews who had come to Scotland several hundred years before Pete was born, and a touch of the dark Irish, who may have been responsible for his large expressive eyebrows. The point, of course, was not a mixture of racial strains, but a brain saturated with the principal intimations of western culture as we knew it in 1950. We did not think then that this multi-cultured concept was developed by white men, and consequently, was false, or inappropriate for use by black. We did not think that longing and jealousy were unique to the ruling class, nor did we suppose that the harmonies of nature sounded as dissonance to the ears of the under-privileged. As to matters politic, we insisted on justice and fairness, without the profound recognition of 1994, that these qualities for people living together were either unobtainable, or so ephemeral that new substitute formulations were necessary. We always have liked to create systems of thought which include answers to problems. Yet we are skeptical about what to do with ideas addressed to problems which are not defined. Throughout this whole century, both skepticism (Watch out "It ain't necessarily so"), and pragmatism ("It's no good unless it works"), were the great American modulations of forces that threatened to enmasse unusual power or to grind too hard against the weak. "Temporizing", that is, keeping the thought from moving too fast or too far, was the more unfortunate aspect of the Twentieth Century mind. Politicians all became tackers, willing to go from the left and then to the right, thinking, perhaps wrongly, that they were moving in a frontal direction. Truth became an irritant, and since it was illusive, rarely stood in the way of men of strong purpose. Pete and I, sitting under the horse chestnut tree, on my family's grounds, discussed these matters with a sense of amusement, rather than anguish. We often sipped wine, ate goodies, or little ham sandwiches that my wife prepared for us as we sat in the half-sun finding us through the trees, told stories, played chess, and shook the tail of the universe. We were for Truman, but not strident against Dewey—we believed that intellegence would keep the country going well; we did not address ourselves to such silly concepts as "I have a better family than you, and thus I should be President of the United States."

Bonnell Phillips

(1940-1957)

onnell Phillips was 6 feet 8 inches tall and in the palm of his hand he could conceal a whole deck of cards. When we walked together down the halls in the Department of Justice in Washington in 1942 and 1943, "Bon" and I were known as "Big" and "Bigger". I have, in my long life, met some men taller than myself, but only in this instance did I have a taller companion.

Outsized men have a consanguinity, a common feeling that doesn't reach consciousness but perhaps may be summarized as a sensation that there is nothing to fear among oversized men. Strength tends to neutralize strength. One is expected to be more powerful than the rest of the world, but the extra tall fraternity knows that there is no truth in it, that the weakness of the oversized is their need to be more tender and charitable than others since they have no obvious excuses for roughness. Their natural enemy is the little man who generally is quick moving, highly aggressive and seeking always to cut down big men at their ankles with a scythe. I am sure that Bon and I shared this tall man feeling and a warm affection which came from knowing that we played unusual roles in life.

Bon had a large head and huge hands. His feet, however, were only size 12, petite in comparison with my 16's. I believe that his body structure showed a glandular disarray; in early years he suffered severely from arthritis, later his digestive system served him poorly, and finally cancer struck him down while he was in his early forties. We talked late at night in each other's homes and came at solutions for problems which did not exist. Once Bon, while working at the Federal Communications Commission, was asked to write a speech for the then Chairman, James Fly. He called me, saying he didn't know how to write a speech and the two of us spent the entire night harvesting clichés out of unfamiliar ground. " The Fly" liked the speech.

On another occasion, Bon discovered that a Table Tennis Championship was taking place in his neighborhood and, remembering my tales of my boyhood successes at table tennis tournaments, entered my name in the lists.

I had been a Table Tennis formidable in my last year at high school, reaching the semi-finals of the First National Championship of the United States

Table Tennis Association. But I had dropped this game, along with most sports when I became a student at Harvard College. Indeed, I had no Ping-Pong table easily available to me for a period of about ten years before this D.C. tournament.

On a hot Friday night in August, I survived three rounds carrying me to the semi-finals Saturday morning. I stayed the night at Bon's house where, until early in the morning, we talked and celebrated my victories. We two giants prepared for the semifinals by drinking between us a case of beer. At about 9:30 a.m. next day I found myself in the semi-finals confronted by a determined player wearing tennis shorts, whom we promptly dubbed "Short Pants" Kaufman.

Short Pants Kaufman was precise and efficient in his stroking. He hit the corners with great rapidity. He mixed up short shots and long. He was, in fact, an accomplished table tennis player. IIe did lack something in power, but this was made up for by his stalwart retrieving. His table tennis game was totally different from mine. I was a slasher and a whammer at a ping pong ball and, when in good form, my strokes often resulted in quick wins. With Kaufman it was often necessary to win a point two or three times; he would return a smash, running back into position and return another in the manner of the great retrievers. I don't think I would have had trouble with Kaufman in my best days. But this was not one of them. In the first game of the best three out of five game match, the edge was to me. I began, however, to feel in my mouth the dreadful taste of warmed-over Schlitz beer. I was reminded that even in strong young men (I was then about 35) the body has some limitations. I was soaked with perspiration before the second set had gone very far. Short Pants Kaufman was about as cool as he could be, and as deliberate in his strokes as a champion. Unfortunately, he did not drive me off easily. The match went the full five sets and even the last set was close. When it was all over, my old friend took me back to his apartment and was of the opinion that we should have a celebration because this was a remarkable demonstration of skill under the handicaps which we had self-imposed. My recollection is, however, that I fled to my home and slept for 24 hours solidly, thanks to my friend's ministrations, and the even more devastating ones administered by Short Pants Kaufman.

As Bon was of heroic size, so too were the stories he told about himself. They took on a dimension somewhat above human stature. For example, Bon reported that in 1932 when he was a student at Yale, he learned to fly an airplane at an airport near New Haven. The plane was an open plane, left over from the first World War. He fastened himself into his seat using a seat belt just as the driver of a modern small car will do. The time came when he became proficient in flying. "Puck" Adams, the light of his life, had a home no more than 15 miles from the airport. It was Bon's practice, once he was able to fly solo, to zoom down over her house announcing his presence by revving his engine. Puck would come out in the porch and wave a handkerchief or a scarf in a loving gesture. In the course of time, Bon mastered many of the stunts such as turning and diving and twisting, which were available to pilots of smaller aircraft. One of these was the Immelman turn, in which the plane describes a vertical circle in the air. Bon was most pleased to have mastered this daring exploit. He flew fervently towards the house of his lady, of whom mention has been made, and went low, revving his motor in anticipation of seeing her emerge on the porch. He would then show off with his Immelman turn. Puck did not come out, having other business that day, and Bon rather dolefully went back to the airport. As he got out of his aircraft, he realized that he had failed to fasten his seat belt and had he pursued his vertical circle over his fiancee's house, there is little doubt that he would have thrown himself into her arms more rapidly than anticipated.

Everything about Bon was big. With his heroic size, he was said to have been a descendant of the great colonial Governor Wendell Phillips, and some said that on the other side of his family he was a direct descendant of Pocahontas and John Smith of the Virginia colonies. I, of course, accepted his

Wendell Phillips inheritance, but gave little credence to the Pocahontas claim.

Bon also told us of an ocean cruise over the Pacific which he and Puck made celebrating their Epithalamion. Bon one night drank much more than was good for him and walked on the deck, in order to breathe in some fresh air, where he saw a heavy rope hanging over the side of the deck. He decided to go down the rope and put his hands in the cool Pacific. He went down the side some 30 or 40 feet when he suddenly realized to his total consternation that he was near the point where the water was washing the large ocean vessel; had he made contact with the water, he doubtless would have been pulled away into the dark night and served as good food for the sharks who cannot always be counted upon to extend professional courtesy to lawyers. Hand over hand in the silence of the night, he climbed up to the deck, pulling himself onto it cold sober.

Bon's last illness was cancer. In 1952, he was treated and died at the National Institute of Health in Bethesda, Maryland. It was still the McCarthy era. The physicians asked Bon a lot of questions, and then asked him if there was anything else he had to say about himself. He responded, "Yes, I am a card carrying member of the Communist Party of the United States and Joe McCarthy stinks." The first part of Bonnell's statement was false and the second part was true. His sense of the comic stayed large to the end.

If I truly believed in the Arab tale of appointment at Sumara, or fatal inevitability, I would suppose that Bon's life and death constituted some evidence for the theory. He did not die when he went over the side of the ocean liner in the middle of the night, He did not die when he flew his open plane without fastening his seat belt, yet all of the man-made remedies could not save him from his dread disease.

At the hospital, Bon was subject to the most modern if ineffectual treatments for cancer. One Wednesday, he called me from his hospital bed at my office in the Department of Justice in New York. He said he was very troubled about his Will and it was at once apparent that he was delirious. He used words like "rent seche", "Hereditaments", "appurtenances", and other words describing ancient forms of possession of real estate. He wanted my advice, he said, as to his Will. I told him I would come on Saturday, flying to Washington early in the morning. Bon replied: "You must come before Friday. I shall die on Friday." I tried to reassure him, to tell him that this was pure nonsense. He died on Friday.

Friday night Puck called me to say that Bon had died. I was subsumed with a sense of guilt, but took out some of the steam from my emotion, as I

sometimes did at this period of my life, by writing
what only magnanimously might be called a poem:

> Bon, old friend, we were about to go,
> carried by plane, but the metal bird
> was slow,
> And that other swooped too fast, the
> grim, black crow
> of Death; Bon, our visit is postponed.

> We have a date to keep in an unknown
> place,
> I don't know the time, the sphere, but
> I know your face,
> And shall seek it proudly, in a split
> of time, in some niche of space.

> Bon, old friend, our plane was slow,
> The Tower cleared yours first to go.

Bucket of Blood

(1942)

I have not purported to make of this volume an autobiography taking me through the brakes and thickets of the practice of law. Here and there, I have mentioned my law practice, but without detail, and only as subsidiary to some other undertaking. Were this an autobiography, stepping on all the stones extruding in the racing river of life, I should have written about Harvard Law School where I spent three not quite idyllic years from 1934-1937. When I emerged from law school at the low point of the depression, my first lawyer's job as a member of the bar was at $12 a week for a lawyer who employed 5 lawyers, and was a leader of what was then called the Labor Bar. He represented labor unions such as the International Ladies Garment Workers Union, and some of the exotica of the New York culture such as Sol Hurok, the great impresario, who, among other activities, represented the Ballet Russe de Monte Carlo. Hurok was a man with whom to conjure, and in his group of artists, there was Vizona, the great Russian exile ballerina. In 1939 when I was enjoying my brief stay at $12 a week at this law office, Vizona had put on a good deal of weight during her summer holiday. This caused an infuriated Hurok to deny her the premier ballet role on opening night for the ballet.

Most of what follows was told to me by Sy Peyser, a classmate of mine from Harvard College who, by coincidence was working with a law firm in the same office building as mine which housed many theatrical personalities, and at this moment in time Peyser's firm represented Vizona. Peyser told me this story at luncheon one day. One day she came rushing down the corridor at the law office where many young lawyers were working, their doors opened to the corridor. Her arms were raised above her, "Feel me! Feel me! Feel me! That Sol Hurok says I am too fat!" Sy assured me that none of the lawyers took advantage of Vizona's gracious offer, but Vizona's father barged into the building about the same day into my suite of offices, where down the corridor his loud voice could be heard demanding that my boss set up a duel with swords between Vizona's father and Sol Hurok. The matter steamed and bubbled for a month or so, until my boss, a superb labor negotiator, solved the problem. He found that a Hollywood company was contemplating producing a film about the life of

Vizona. What better casting could there be than to have Vizona herself playing the leading role; moreover, at a price exquisitely large? Vizona, who had already begun to diet to avoid future disaster, eagerly accepted the job, and all the money, while Hurok, without paying damages, was able to place a beautiful young star in Vizona's ballet place. I believe she was Maria Tallchief, a glorious American Indian dancer, but I am not sure.

This office was a mere way station on the road to Washington D.C., where New Dealers were sharpening their wits in an effort to save our capital structure. In the perverse irony of history, the efforts headed by FDR, sometimes called by Republicans a "traitor to his class" were branded as "Socialist or Communist". One could almost see the aristocratic Roosevelt sitting on his yacht off the coast of Maine, under a nautical cap provided by Abercrombie & Fitch, in white flannels, smoking a cigarette in a long holder while plotting the overthrow of the system. But what the system was, comrade, no one seemed to be able to say either on the Right or the Left. There are right wing conservatives, who, even today, looking back over the vaulted arch of history to the 1930's, think that Roosevelt, with his improvisations and his tinkering, and his heroic efforts to save the banks from failure, the farmers from lack of electricity, the poor from lack of housing and the old and ill from destruction and despair was communistic. And because myths occupy the human spirit far more than reality, to some, FDR is still known as an arch political devil, even though he guided us to victory through two great wars on the Atlantic and Pacific, the most terrifying this country has ever known, and pulled this nation out of depression.

I soon went to Washington and first to the National Labor Relations Board, which was furthering the objectives of the Wagner Act. Monsignor Jon A. Ryan told the House that he regarded the Wagner Act as "the most important legislation enacted, not only for labor, but for democracy since we began enacting federal legislation in this country." Many seemed to agree with him at the time, although with the passage of decades he seems to have overestimated its value, particularly since labor unions are no longer important forces to reckon with in our country. I wrote about this excitement of effervescent accomplishment in a book called *Government Lawyer* published in 1956. Without attempting to retread my steps as reported in *Government Lawyer*,[2] but in order to convey some of the strong feelings engendered by the attempt to work out social problems through the activity of government I am, repeating a substantial part of a chapter from *Government Lawyer* called "Bucket of Blood".

After writing many decisions for the Board and later writing many briefs, I was assigned to "Matter

---

[2] A book very well received by its few readers, and offered for sale by The Lawyers Heritage on a list of outstanding treatises and biographies by American lawyers.

of Jacob Brothers," a trial which was coming on to be heard in Hancock, a little town in Western Maryland, not far from the West Virginia Frontier.

The International Ladies Garment Worker's Union had complained to the Board that when it sought to organize a uniform factory in Hancock a hostile anti-union demonstration had taken place, the union organizers had been run out of town and eight or nine ladies who had had the temerity to join the union had been summarily discharged.

I proceeded to Hancock by automobile, taking an historic route followed by the retreating armies of the Potomac through Germantown and Frederick where Stonewall Jackson touched not a hair of yon gray head, and on past several bloody battlefields to the little town of Hancock more recently scarred by a different kind of battle.

I established myself at a boardinghouse whose genial proprietor had sympathized with the factory girls who had joined the union. I was not there long when I was visited by a newspaper reporter of 20 who fancied himself a rural Heywood Broun. (Broun was a brilliant, independent maverick journalist who wrote a daily column called "It Seems to Me" for several hundred newspapers.) He knew a great deal about the demonstration which had driven the organizers away, about which of the blades in the town had participated in it, and he gave me his enthusiastic cooperation. As I conducted interviews with various townspeople, I became aware of the intense hostility addressed not only to the union but to the United States Government, as it was represented through me, a National Labor Relations Board lawyer.

I reached Hancock one cold spring day in 1942 a week before the hearing was scheduled in order thoroughly to prepare for the trial.

Venison sold in the restaurant for 35 cents and was featured at each meal, since the men of the community found it easy to shoot deer on the mountainside close to town. Each morning it was a common sight to see young buck tied to the roofs of cars slowly rolling down Main Street. The mountain did more than support the deer; it was said that in season its slopes were lush with Mackintosh apples, that many men of the town picked the apples and lived in mountainside barracks where they were voluntarily confined from Monday through Friday when they were paid off and released. Upon their release, it was reported to me, most of these men headed straight for the local saloon which was dubbed, "A Bucket of Blood," because it was said that rarely a Friday night passed without someone's blood flowing on the floor. In the age of the New Deal, a community only 95 miles from Washington could retain in so many ways a feudal form of life, which I supposed had passed from America 100 years before.

I learned that the bitterness expressed to the union and of which I partook - was due to the circumstance that most of the wage-earning males of the community had lost their employment some 15 years earlier because of an ill-fated strike of the Brotherhood of Railroad Trainmen against the Railroad. Before the strike the Railroad had maintained a siding at Hancock which had been a hive of employment, and in order to break the strike it had diverted the work elsewhere along its lines.

The men were opposed to unions because they attributed their personal tragedies to the Brotherhood. The community itself offered little opportunity for gainful employment until a New York uniform manufacturer moved his factory to the town. He had been given inducement to come to Hancock in the form of a favorable lease and other aid from the local merchants who were interested in building up the community.

Nearly half the women of the community worked at the factory and supported their families at a level of earnings shocking to an effete lawyer from the big city. The factory, before its difficulties with the Labor Board, had had difficulties with the Wage and Hour Administration because its scales were below the minimum provided by the statute in those days. And if my recollection does not fail me, that minimum was 30 cents an hour. But the employment was steady, the air was clean, the homes were mostly comfortable even if old; there was a little local movie house and the food, in the restaurants at least, was inexpensive and plentiful.

I visited, however, a factory girl of about 25 who lived with her aged mother in a tar-papered box heated by a small potbellied stove. I noticed that here and there the walls had been reinforced with corrugated cardboard and, in several places, by magazine covers in symmetrical piles neatly glued together.

In many ways the town had dignity. The people with whom I spoke were direct and to the point. They were sincere in their dislike for organized labor.

The "facts" as they were later reconstructed, were that the ILGWU had appointed an elderly woman of early American stock and rural background as its organizer for Hancock. She had come to the town, established herself in the boarding-house where I was later to reside and secretly talked to some of the women working at the factory. Within a few weeks her influence spread, and after dark women came to her and covertly signed union cards. Then, when the time was ripe, the union sent a male organizer to help her.

By this time the secret was out and the town reacted as violently as if enemy agents had been discovered in City hall. One morning the power was cut at the factory and the mayor of the town and the president of the local bank addressed the girls at work. The burden of their remarks was: "Don't join the union or the factory will move away." Shortly afterward, in accordance with a pre-arranged signal, worked out with the telephone company, the voluntary fire department sounded its sirens and most of the men of the community gathered outside the factory gates where the union organizers were accosted, forced into their automobiles, and escorted by a procession of cars to the city limits. The organizers were warned not to return under penalty of more violent treatment.

At about the same time some of the women who had been most active in organizing the union were discharged. These facts came out slowly in the course of the government's testimony.

Before the testimony started I was to fear that identification as an attorney for the United States was not a passport sufficient to assure protection in this medieval duchy.

I had moved from the boarding house to the local hotel where the manager was most reluctant to accept me, indicating that he could not guarantee my safety. Apart from this, his hotel afforded little of the attractions which Americans have learned to associate with that pleasant word. If it was not a flea house in the literal sense of the word it looked like one. It had no central plumbing. Next to my ancient bed was a broken water pitcher and an old porcelain basin.

By the time I signed the register I had been joined by a young man recently hired by the Baltimore

Office of the Board and inanely sent to me to achieve by observation some trial experience. The hostility of the community worked on him even more rapidly than upon myself and I was not and am not now, with Generals Marshall and Eisenhower, among the heroes of modern times.

We quickly moved from the hotel to a far more luxurious resort in Berkeley Springs, across the West Virginia line, which attracted during season a large following tasting the magical waters of the area. However, this was not the season for drinking nostrums, and the furniture of the sprawling hotel was covered with cloths. The hotel apparently had no other guests except Board's counsel, union's counsel, the company's counsel and the trial examiner, an elderly man who had once been hung in effigy at Weirton, West Virginia.

No sooner had we reached our asylum in West Virginia when the young edition of Heywood Broun telephoned to report that as the hearing started next morning it was the intention of some of the young blades of the town to unload buckshot in the general direction of the attorneys, the trial examiner and the witnesses. The threat seemed menacing because the hearing was to take place in the movie theatre, an old barn with a stage at one end and a solitary combined entrance and exit at the other. Our plans were that the trial examiner and the stenographer would sit at a desk on the stage where there would also be a chair for the witness.

Counsel, with their backs turned towards the rear of the theatre, would stand just before the elevated stage while addressing their questions to the witnesses. According to our informant, it was the plan of the young men, hatched at the "Bucket of Blood" during that evening, to bring their guns through the sole entrance, unload the buckshot in the direction of the stage and beat a hasty departure. This information was not calmly received. My young associate seemed even more troubled than I. He took me to my room and said he thought the hearing ought to be canceled, and while I bravely attempted to lessen the impact of our information, he assured me that violence would take place and that he was certain of it because of his experience with the psychology of a lynching mob.

Then, while the room seemed to spin and my stomach grew sick, he told me that I could not really understand what was happening unless I, too, had once pulled the rope around the throat of a "Nigger." He explained that he had gone to law school in the town of Athens, Georgia, where he had partaken in a lynching and had himself had some direct contact with the rope.

I raced from my assistant, whose panic doubtless had to keep company with his sense of guilt, to the room of the trial examiner. The trial examiner was a distinguished man who, I believe, was then approaching 70, somewhat hard of hearing, and he, too, had experienced violence of a different sort.

He had been the trial examiner presiding over the stormy Weirton Steel proceedings. He had been forced to move these proceedings from Weirton to Steubenville, Ohio, out of prudence and a decent respect for his own safety and the safety of others. He said to me something about the young being brash and being willing to take chances. He urged that I make an effort to furnish adequate protection to the lawyers and all concerned when the hearing opened the next morning.

It was almost midnight when I telephoned to the Regional Director of the Board who was a stranger to me. He at first thought me a timid soul who had given too much emphasis to town gossip. But upon the assurance of the other lawyers, fortunately lodged in the same hotel, that the threat seemed to be a serious one, he undertook to provide protection. Within an hour he reported that he had roused the governor who had promised that the state police would be present in the hearing room at 10 a.m.

Unfortunately the hearing was scheduled for 9:30 a.m. In the middle of the night, I knocked at the door of the trial examiner to assure him that the state troopers would protect us. My knocks were answered by a tired voice inquiring who I was. Upon his satisfaction that I was I, I heard the sounds of furniture being moved away from the door, and when it was opened I found the examiner, much shaken, sitting fully clad on a chair. My assurances were not sufficient to restore serenity because the examiner was troubled about the half hour interval between the hearings opening and the arrival of the promised protection. I assured him that even deer hunters would not go after greater game at 9:30 in the morning, that such violence would require first a visit to the saloon which did not open so early in the morning, and that the United States could well take a risk for half an hour. He thought any risk unnecessary as it was made apparent to me that the old cling to life even more tenderly than the young.

Next morning, we did not start quite promptly, but some time before 10 the trial examiner took his seat on the stage; the witness sat near by him and I advanced with knocking knees to start my questioning. I felt that the trial examiner was not paying attention to the testimony, and it seemed that his face was blanched, when suddenly a big smile fired over it. The union's lawyers handed me a paper upon which was written, "The state troopers are here." I pivoted about, and in the rear of the room, blocking access to the theatre, stood six huge and comforting state troopers, armed not only with revolvers, but with rifles. The blood returned to the examiner's face while my knees grew steady.

Later that day as the testimony progressed, the State Commissioner of Labor entered the hearing room and represented to us that his presence alone would ensure the safety of us all. It was not without some misgivings that we released the state troopers. The State Commissioner was as good as his word; the most menacing episode during the hearing occurred one evening after another Board attorney and I had interrogated a young woman involved in the labor dispute. Her rejected suitor had become convinced that our questioning was not solely along business lines. Fortunately his jealous mind had not yet fabricated an illusion clearly designating which of us longed for his woman. Not knowing whom to punch, he challenged us to fight him separately, an invitation we were able to decline. Under these circumstances, our credentials as representatives of the government bore some weight.

We had been let off lightly. In another NLRB matter a field investigator had faced a revolver and had avoided being shot only by submerging the weapon in an inspired cascade of appealing words.

The government's case was convincing. The company had discharged all of the girls most active in organizing the union. the honesty of the townspeople prevented any obscuring of what had taken place during the mass demonstration in which the organizers were driven out of town. As a shot in the dark, I called the local banker to the stand. After he admitted that he had urged the girls not to join the union on penalty that the company would move away from Hancock, I asked him about the company's tenancy at the plant. It developed that the banker was himself the landlord, and he volunteered to fetch a copy of the lease. He forthrightly read into the record a provision of the lease which gave to the company the right to terminate its tenancy in the event there was labor trouble.

Near the close of the government's case, there was little doubt that we had been successful. There remained, however, one woman to be examined whose story vexed me. She was far too good a witness—each time I questioned her her recollection of events taking place at the plant grew fuller and more precise. She could corroborate things that were said to the other girls that were important to the case—anti-union incidents which took place at the plant prior to the discharges and demonstration, and her testimony would support not only her own case but would put the clincher to most of the others. Throughout the four or five days of presentation of the government's case, she sat raptly attentive in the first row. Each night I spoke to her and each night her story grew.

Finally, an important Labor Board attorney on a trip of inspection to the field stopped by to audit the proceedings. I asked him to talk with Mrs. Doe, and he reported that he had never seen a better prepared witness and could not appreciate my qualms in putting her on the stand. At my insistence, he interrogated her on the stand himself and her story was a lalapalooza. There was excitement in the courtroom. Defendant's counsel broadcasted surprise as he began his cross-examination. He proceeded rather aimlessly to introduce a time-card which demonstrated that Mrs. Doe had last been in the employ of the company a week before the union organizer had first come to Hancock. The hearing then recessed for luncheon.

The time-card ravaged my confidence. I took Mrs. Doe aside at the luncheon and told her that if she were lying she had better speak the truth now. At first she claimed that the defendant was suppressing another time-card which would show her employment during the next two-weeks' period when the critical events took place. Then she broke down, confessing that she had made it all up, and that she had been laid off because of a squabble with her supervisor at a time before there was any talk of organizing the union. She also said that she had become friendly with the union organizer immediately upon her arrival in Hancock.

Later both had agreed that her case might as well be thrown in with the others and had conspired in fabricating her persuasive story. After listening to her friends testify it became an easy matter for Mrs. Doe to take the stand and corroborate them in minute detail.

I think at that moment I first grew aware of the limitations inherent in the fact-finding process. I was young and I was indignant. Upon my return to the courtroom I was prepared to make a statement to the trial examiner in which I would ask that the complaint as addressed to Mrs. Doe be dismissed and inform the examiner in open court that Mrs. Doe was lying.

By doing so I was taking the risk that the rest of the case, in which I had the fullest confidence, might be prejudiced for if one of the Board's witnesses was a perjurer that fact might cast a cloud of suspicion over the testimony of all.

As I entered the court room after the recess I was collared by defendant's attorney who spoke somewhat as follows: "I am amazed at the strength of the Government's case, and had I realized what the 'facts' were I would never have permitted the case to come to trial. If there is any concession you can offer me, I am sure that my client will now accept a settlement, rather than putting in his defense."

Of course, I eagerly offered a concession which was the striking of the allegations concerning Mrs. Doe from the complaint, and I informed my adversary of my luncheon conversation with her. He smiled and graciously told me that if he had remained ignorant of the confession he would not have continued cross-examination about the meaning of the time-card he had introduced into evidence, because the inconsistency between the card and the witness' testimony was so great that he, too, thought his client had suppressed a second time-card which covered the pertinent working period.

All the other ladies, except for Mrs. Doe, were reinstated with full back pay, and so far as is known to me, as a result of the Board's decision, both the union and the factory remained in Hancock to the contentment of some if not all of the citizenry.

I since have had occasion to reflect how often in Labor Board proceedings and generally in the proceedings of courts, perjury passed unidentified gracefully clad in the robes of truth. It is of vital importance that all who deal with the processes of courthouse justice should be on constant guard that they are presenting reasonable approximations of what took place rather than pure fancy or deceit. A lawyer desiring to win his cause will normally present for consideration that testimony which most colorfully seems to support his position. A lawyer becomes critical usually only when his witness is hostile or takes him by surprise.

In my law school days I read Jerome Frank's LAW AND THE MODERN MIND, a book which pulled at the deep roots of legal thought and exposed the fact that there is no certainty in law and that only minds which hunger for father-symbols in society would suspect to find certainty there. In further books and articles culminating in COURTS ON TRIAL, Judge Frank pitilessly exposed the weaknesses of the fact-finding process as well as the difficulties and uncertainties in finding or creating an applicable principle or rule to be applied to the "facts" as they are found by the trier of facts. Had I not eaten lunch with Mrs. Doe, the "fact" of the Hancock case necessarily would have been that Mrs. Doe was discriminatorily discharged by the company and entitled to reinstatement with back pay. Moreover, since the defendant had not intended to explore the impact of the time-card upon her direct testimony, there can be little doubt that the Circuit Court of Appeals would have sustained such a finding which would have become final for all eternity.

Judge Frank's thinking about the fact-finding process like that of Mr. Justice Holmes, has been attacked as leading to justification for a materialistic, cynical approach to the law. Nothing could be further from fact. An awareness of the tentativeness of human judgment, of the imaginative speculation which is needed to give moral form to the workings of society is what in the last analysis, Judge Frank called for in his writings. He destroyed nothing that a modern mind can accept rationally, and he opened the gates to new horizons for the improvement of the judicial and fact-finding processes.

We know today that if there is a "natural" law we are powerless to understand it because we have only an imperfect knowledge of nature's workings. What I deem "natural law" you may be positive is "unnatural law." We know today that the courts do not administer "God's law" because, among other reasons, the laws are frequently devised and implemented by godless men. It is related that an Illinois attorney, charged with a wrong, approached the bench and fervently asserted that he was represented not only by himself but by God. The judge is said to have replied, "God is not a member of the bar of Cook county or of the State of Illinois. Leave for him to appear as counsel is denied."

We know that the "law" is not written in the Constitution, in papers, articles, or even books like Blackstone, since papers do not sit as judges or juries and men have different concepts of the meaning and application of written words. We must, therefore, conclude that the "law" is what happens to a litigant who uses the machinery of "law," that is to say that the "law" is that John Smith owes Tom Brown $100 only when a court of last resort has so decided. This is the teaching of Judge Frank, as I interpret it, and this is also a doctrine which gives fair promise of elevating the status of a lawyer, or a judge, or a legislator, into that of the practitioner of creative art. For lawyers, judges and the like are dabblers in a plastic medium where there are no limitations of knowledge such as those imposed by the physical sciences, where there are no social "facts" to serve as correlates to physical "facts." There may be only one way known to make a steam locomotive run efficiently. There may be a thousand ways available to run society efficiently but none of them is known. The lawyers' work in litigation, in decision, in legislation, is with the content of our political and social structure and the outcome of their work represents their energy, their imagination, their skill, and, vastly more important, the moral affirmations which they impose upon their doings.

To the extent that lawyers try to extend or create or affirm doctrine which is consistent with the form of our great and emerging democracy, our democracy survives, notwithstanding the pressures from within and without that seek to destroy it. To the extent that lawyers are indifferent to the doctrinal aspects of our democracy, which include, among many others, the concept of fair play[3] or even-handed treatment for all, our democracy will slip away without our knowing it. For it is the lawyers, who sometimes function as judges or as legislators, who have the power to mold and change our society. There have been more revolutions bloodlessly waged in the decisions of the courts, and in the legislation of Congress than ever took place on the battlefield.

The need for moral affirmation in the practice of law was thrust upon me somewhere in the vicinity of "A Bucket of Blood," and it has been reinforced by the inspiring teachings of Judge Frank.

* * * *

---

[3] I have searched and cannot find "fair play" in the Constitution.

The British Are Coming

In the year 1959, I summoned up my courage to practice law on my own. I left a sizable firm, to occupy a small office at 285 Madison Avenue, New York City, a building dominated by the presence of a large advertising agency which occupied most of the floors. Greenbaum, Wolff & Ernst, and I, as its counsel, were lawyers whose space could not long survive the incursion of the advertisers. My rooms were separate from the firm's, but we had a loose association as much based upon friendship as upon advantage. I had a small library of my own, a secretary and a brilliant assistant. My doughty little group faced the world of law firms growing larger each day and forcing the little fellows to become more and more dependent upon the good will and interfacing of their clients.

The arrival of the British lawyers in New York in 1959, courtesy of the American Bar Association, brought me a new turn of life. The ABA had requested of its members that we offer hospitality to the British lawyers who were venturing to New York for one of the frequently held love fests between the two bars, based upon a cunning lawyer's notion that the two bars are similar because they have in common the common law. It should be noted at once that we have the common law in common but very little else and in this country increasingly little of the common law, but both countries allocate tax deductions for professional meetings.

A British barrister becomes a barrister by passing a written examination after some organized study of law at the undergraduate level. Thus, he is awarded the LLB degree and not the J.D. common in this country, which connotes that law is a graduate study. To qualify for practice, the Brit is required to do two important things:

(a) find himself a pupilage with a barrister, and (b) find himself a tenancy in the restricted real estate available for this purpose in the Inns of Court. If he can do that and attend a certain number of dinners at his Inn, and subject himself to a considerable amount of verbal hazing of the most grandiloquent, but non-abusive kind, he may emerge a barrister ready to receive briefs through the intermediation of the Clerk of Chambers. And he can only go to Court if he has a brief given him by a Solicitor who has worked out fee arrangements with Almighty Clerk. Until recent decades, the fees owed to the barrister were placed in a slit pocket in the back of the barrister's robe. The slit is still there, but no longer used, and its name almost unknown.

I went for the first time to the Law Courts of London with my friend, Peter Downe, who had a 10:00 o'clock trial. At 9:55 we left Chambers and hurriedly reached the courthouse across the Strand where Peter raced for the robing room. There, an ancient attendant had Peter's robe out and ready to slip over his shoulders, having taken the trouble to learn in advance who was to be in Court that morning. With one hand, Peter slapped his wig on top of his head and without breaking his stride, turned from the robing room to the courtroom where he arrived precisely at the nick of 10:00, pulling from his briefcase a note which described the case that had been prepared by the solicitor — the British barrister normally does not consult with clients at all.

Peter said he was ready for the plaintiff, and, indeed, he was. In a skillful medley of questions, he drew from the plaintiff the basics of the story of a middle-aged man who, grazed by one car, stumbled forward, and was hit by another. The plaintiff was not cross-examined and within a few minutes Peter had put on a corroborative witness who was ineffectively cross-examined. Then Peter rested the case, having presented all his facts having to do with the merits. What I saw were complicated issues of causation of injury, and I suppose that it would have taken two or three days to bring in that case in the New York Supreme Court. Defendant had a sole witness whom Peter sharply cross-examined. The matter of extent of damages had been separated for later hearing, if necessary. The summations of counsel were both gems and since the case was tried without a jury, the judge, upon completion of the summations, at once announced his decision, making comments about the evidence. We were out of the courthouse by 11:30 a.m. and Peter was successful. Since the solicitor had prepared the case, Peter had done almost no independent preparation, and I was introduced with considerable pleasure to the administration of justice in an expeditious form. Similarities between the Americans and the UK barristers are not close.

But all this is a digression from the beginning of my friendships with the British Bar. Peter Downe was present in my house at a function which included some 30 or more British lawyers responsive to the request of the American Bar made in 1959; so was Lord Roger Nathan and his wife, Penelope, with whom my wife and I became friends and who later became Lord Mayor of London. There were Scotch and Welsh lawyers present. One from the Isle of Ismay, which is celebrated for having produced a single malt scotch much favored in British clubs.

Peter Downe and I became fast friends. I showed him New York during the next few days and before he had left for England he had decided, partly as a result of the prodding of my friend, Morris Ernst, to collaborate with me on a simple book describing the lawyer customs of the two countries. The book would not be scholarly but would give to American and British lawyers a concept of the two bars in action. We corresponded, drew up an outline and Peter quickly went to work on the book. I lasted very little beyond the outlining and a few beginning pages of text. Within a few months, I was in England and the following year he was back in New York again, but the book remained unwritten.

In a few years we both had stopped writing this book. I was given the dread news that Peter, 43 years old, who had survived perilous action in World War II, had been killed in an auto accident. He owned an MG sports car, in which were crowded Patricia, his wife, two of his children, and the dog. When traveling at high speed, the car hit some small object in the road, jumped the curb and landed in a privet hedge. The rest of the family was unscathed, but Peter was slumped dead behind the wheel. The dog was missing three days, and was found some 40 feet away stuck in the hedge, apparently none the worse for his confinement. I was singularly moved by Peter's death and dismayed that we had failed in our joint project. I determined to do something in place of it and wrote to the Head of Peter's Chambers, Elwyn Jones, asking him to find for me some young barrister who wanted to be educated in American legal customs and who could be imported to the United States for the summer at my expense. In this way, the younger lawyers in my small office learned a great deal about British practice, and the British lawyer, by participating in ours, learned even more about the American analogue. Years later, Mary Auld, a dear friend of the Downes', took us to an Eleventh Century cathedral, where, in an ancient graveyard, I read Peter's headstone. The next stone mentioned a lawyer dead more than 500 years.

The first barrister who came to us under this dispensation was Tony MacNeile, a handsome young Englishman of distinguished ancestry. What he saw and accomplished in the States earned him many a dinner on his return to London. He lived in our Riverdale home and I drove him each day back and forth with me. His mother, who was a lady in waiting for the Queen, frequently wrote, warning him against gangsters on the streets of New York and urging him to take maximum defensive measures. One noon on our way to luncheon, we rounded the corner of Madison Avenue and 41st Street when, to Tony's astonishment, we were confronted with two New York City policemen, guns drawn, running through an office building doorway next to the corner. We, in turn, ducked into the next doorway on the theory that if bullets were fired, it would be better not to be in their line. A few minutes later, the police re-emerged, escorting with them a handcuffed citizen who did not seem to be enjoying his lunch hour. Tony, who had been in New York only a few days when this happened, announced that he would be able to command more than one dinner telling that story. As it went, he must have earned many a dinner through his spectacular adventures in the United States.

One weekend, we took him to the country house of friends on the shore of Long Island Sound. They possessed a speedboat: and a young daughter very agile in the use of water skis, who made it her mission to teach Tony how to use the skis. That Sunday afternoon, Tony was placed on the skis but could not quite master the process of standing erect, which is accomplished through a sudden forward lurch as the tension against the waves grows sufficient to help support the skier. The boat sped off, the skier in trail, but ten times Tony faltered, plunging into the sea. Courageously, he rose and like Neptune, trident in hand, water draining past his head and shoulders, he went on the skis again. But at the end of the tenth failure, our host, the pilot of the speedboat and a physician, declined to let Tony do it again. We were all bemused by this demonstration of British courage. Tony, emerging from the water somewhat battered, was, of course, given the proper relief, a single malt scotch from the Island of Ismay.

The summer following Tony MacNeile's picaresque adventures in the United States and in my law office, Elwyn Jones wrote to me suggesting that I bring into my law office the son of a solicitor and a bright young barrister, named Christopher Symons. I did so, and, as in the case of Tony, Christopher spent his summer in my home in Riverdale. Tony himself returned during the summer, so I had two barristers working in my office.

Christopher was a remarkable young lawyer. He was very careful about detail and quick to learn. He kept writing in his notebook the names of people he met and used writing as a vital daily supplement to memory. I sent him on a mission to take deposition testimony in Akron, Ohio, in a case in which we represented some ship repairers on the Great Lakes. They had a monopoly claim against the American Shipping Company, the owner of a fleet of steamships, which seemed to control ship repairs on the Great Lakes through the device of moving their patronage from one repairer to another. It was a complicated question of American restraint of trade, but Christopher learned the issues quickly. His legal talents were superb and he is today a QC, but his versatility caused wonderment in my law office. We lived at that time in a place which among other points of enjoyment had a tennis court. In my law office, there was an over-proud young lawyer from Connecticut who claimed to be a tennis champion. He had a powerful forehand which was almost unreturnable. Christopher casually mentioned to me that he had almost made the Junior Davis Cup in the UK and used to play tennis with John Lloyd, who later became the UK champion. I contemplated a match between the Connecticut blowhard and the almost Junior Cupper. The match did indeed take place. Christopher was a superb tennis player and unrelenting in his playing. My local champion was not heard to speak of his tennis skills until months after Christopher returned to England.

I confess that during the 1970s and 1980s, I became somewhat of an Anglophile as a result of the friendships I had made with British lawyers. I was invited by a chamber of barristers from the Middle Temple to be their U.S. representative, and I, in turn, arranged for them to be my U.K. representatives. Consequently, I became a door tenant in the Lamb Building and they appeared on the directory of my office building and upon my letterhead. This resounding association led to a trickle of professional work between the two organizations, but primarily served to solidify our friendly relationships.

Keeping Up With the Joneses, Lord and Lady

At the same time, my friendship grew with Elwyn-Jones, QC, then Head of Chambers in the Lamb Building in Middle Temple. I first met him at his residence in Gray's Inn Square, that enormous Inn Court with a magnificent green, where Elwyn and Polly, his multi-gifted wife, maintained an apartment. He was on the cobblestone path waiting for my taxi and I was at once overwhelmed by the British barrister in its most gifted form. At first glance, his brown Bond Street suit looked better than anything in the windows of Brooks, and his well-shined matching shoes represented the British leatherworks at their best. His face was full of bushy eyebrows, but molded in a mischievous rather than in a Mephistophelean bend. The hair still on his head served as a tonsure sufficiently outlining a massive forehead, set off by the high round cheekbones and nose, giving prominence to the small, canny, almost beady eyes which twinkled as he talked.

The hair curled around the back of his head, adding to the projection of his geniality. As soon as he spoke, one knew the presence of a forensic master. We seemed instantly to like each other and I was more or less stunned by the swift wit, hospitality and grace of this sensational Englishman. He had quickly risen from Head of Chambers to Treasurer of Gray's Inn (American equivalent is President) to Attorney General of the United Kingdom from 1964 to 1970, and then, with the return to power of the Labour Party in 1974, to Lord Chancellor, the highest post that non-royalty can hold in the UK, with the possible exception of Prime Minister. Indeed, under English law it is, or has been until very recently, treason, punishable by disembowelment, to kill the King or Queen or the Lord Chancellor, but no one else.

The enormous scope of responsibility imposed upon the Lord Chancellor includes the keeping of the great seal needed to be applied to all laws, the keeping of the King's or Queen's conscience, the guardianship of idiots, the presiding over the House of Lords, and the High Court when that House sits as a Court, the appointment of judges and of Queen's counsel. He opens the court sessions in colorful proceedings and is a member of the Cabinet. There are many other duties, one of the most arduous of which is to live in an ancient apartment in the House of Lords, where there is a spare Woolsack, a dark hallway full of life-size portraits, and where the majesty of England is heavy, indeed. A peerage goes with the office. Sir Elwyn became Baron Elwyn-Jones of Llanelli in the County of Carmarthen and Newham in Greater London. For scholars with underlying intense interest in British customs, it may be noted that the territorial reference in this title refers to his birthplace in Wales, and the reference to Newham to the constituency he represented during the 30 years when he was a member of the House of Commons.

When not in power, Elwyn-Jones served as the principal spokesman in the House of Commons on legal and judicial matters for the shadow cabinet of the Labour Party, another British institution unknown here.

His father was a tinsmith in Llanelli, a small Welsh town, and Elwyn went on to college because of his eleventh year success on examination, a point where intelligence and learning can shatter class privilege. He went first to the University of Wales and later on to Cambridge, where he was a first scholar and president of the Cambridge Union. He was called to the Bar in 1935, thereafter he served in the Second World War, from 1943-1945 with the Royal Artillery in North Africa, Sicily, and Italy, learning something of bullets flying, and the blood and death of combat. Later in the war, he was designated a Major and Deputy Judge Advocate, and in 1945 he became one of the British prosecution counsel at the war trials of Nuremberg. He sometimes talked to us of those trials and his impressions of the Nazi war criminals whose very names created in me a sense of horror. He was able to describe the character of men by a statement of facts so salient that it was unnecessary for him to conclude that they were evil.

When he returned to England, he was elected to Parliament and served in various offices of the Crown. Later on, he, like Lord Arnold Goodman, of whom I have much to say elsewhere, was asked to try to solve the Rhodesian situation and participated in talks in Salisbury, looking towards the settlement that never took place.

Elwyn Jones was my friend during the last twenty years of the meteoric rise depicted above, and thereafter. I was privileged to share with him his points of view about social, personal and legal matters as our families became extensions of each other.

Morris Ernst and I had put out little pamphlets called "Back and Forth". My friends had those collected by Peter Pauper Press in a book as a birthday present for me. "Back and Forth" covered only such temporal and causal matters which were able to incite me into writing.

Elwyn read "Back and Forth" while he was vacationing in Provence from his new duties as Attorney General of U.K. In May of 1968 Martin

Luther King had been assassinated. In one of the pamphlets, I had asked that the accused be tried "through a civilized unbiased act of reason". To this Elwyn observed, in respect of another tragedy,

"When the assassin managed to escape to England I was as A.G. involved in the question of his extradition (in the event he did not agree to return voluntarily). Immediately he got to England an American Weekly - Newsweek I think - published a detailed account of his sordid and criminal activities. I threatened contempt proceedings unless the edition was at once withdrawn. This was done. As extradition proceedings were pending at the time I would undoubtedly have taken them to Court. This was done in respect of the Sunday Times, which published the antecedents of Michael [Malcolm] X just before his trial. The publisher was fincd L5,000." Wc don't restrain the Press and even let trials take place before television cameras. Elwyn went on: "So we did our best to stop trial by newspaper developing. The fact that Malcolm X is now charged with a particularly cruel murder in the West Indies is yet another illustration of the fact that important legal principles are often founded on the least worthy of cases."

England had turned out administrative tribunals setting up an industrial relations court which did not work within the system of robed judges and barristers. Elwyn observed that "the Tory Government has created a court mechanism which requires the Industrial Relations Court to determine wholly political issues and in the same enforcement section requires The court to accept the ipse dixit of a Minister on what really are justiciable issues. That which is political has to be decided judicially. That which is judicial is to be determined politically. The result is an almost total refusal by our 10 million Trade Unionists to accept the authority of this specially created branch of the High Court. The attempt of the Judge to make the court acceptable by not appearing in a wig and gown has been a total failure. As one docker put it to me - "I resent being sent to prison by a man in a lounge suit".

But this had been the American development. Administrative agencies multiplied as the Congress, with increasing frequency, after the turn of the Century acted on the belief that special statutes were needed to right almost every wrong. Men in this country sat everywhere in business suits deciding questions of fact and law and the late Judge Jerome Frank wrote a book entitled "If Men Were Angels" designed to prove that black Mother Hubbards were not necessary in the discharge of judicial functions.

We now became correspondents, writing frequently and we began to visit each other's homes. Sir Elwyn was not yet Lord Chancellor, but he was a Bencher sitting at the head table at Gray's Inn. A number of times I, too, became a Bencher sitting next to him surrounded by dignitaries of the Bar and the Bench while the members of Gray's Inn sat along the sides of a great "U". At the very ends of this "U" were the students who at any moment were subject to possible verbal hazing.

Back of the dining room at Gray's Inn was a small room equipped for the administration of Bloody Marys and other necessities for the continued good life of the Benchers. It was here that I was able to observe quasi-judicial forms of life at their most pleasant moments.

After considerable correspondence about an American holiday I met Lord Elwyn Jones on August 7, 1974, at the British Airlines Building at JFK at or about 4:00 p.m. I parked my car, courtesy of the British Consulate (parking, not Lincoln), at the arrival drive in front of the terminal. We were assisted by Mr. Baker, head of the terminal, and by a representative of the Consulate's office, a Mr. Tom Chapman. No great concern was shown by the airport personnel for his Lordship's safety nor did I detect the presence of any security people.

I drove Elwyn home and we started our holiday together. Anna prepared a recognizably delicious dinner which was accompanied with a Chateau

Ducru Beaucailloux 1966 which had been sent to me by Mr. Francois Boire, the owner of the Chateau, who had dined with us a few months before.[4] Elwyn was delighted with the dinner and the wine and the view from the terrace; we were fairly early to bed since he was functioning on his Welsh timeclock.

On Thursday, August 8, we arose early and had a swim, lolled around on the terrace, thence to town where we listened to the trial of the Rothko case for less than an hour and then had lunch with Judge Millard Midonick, whose case it was,[5] Judge Edelstein, Judge Tenny, Judge Stewart, Judge Pierce, and Judge Bauman at the Merchants Club; thence to my offices where Elwyn met my colleagues and chatted with them for, perhaps, three-quarters of an hour; whereupon we returned to Riverdale for a change of clothes, a return to midtown and a drink at the Harvard Club with General Telford Taylor. If you think that Samuel Pepys was a detailed autobiographer, savor this day with the Lord Chancellor which I carefully noted in August 1974. Still on August 8th, the Lord Chancellor, Anna, Millard Midonick[6] and I to the Algonquin for

---

[4] By way of continued irrelevancy, we received Francis Xavier Boire, son of the celebrated vintner, as a house guest early in 1974. The Chateau bottle had a photograph of the huge chateau. Francis, then 16 years old, pointed to a single window near one end of the photograph on the bottle, "I live there".

[5] He had to put judicial price tags on a most advanced form of American art.

[6] My friend since high schoold days.

dinner — good roast beef — followed by a trip to the Palace Theatre where we saw Carol Channing in Lorelei. Home late and a nightcap and so to sleep.

On Friday the 9th, Elwyn gardened a little and took in the Hoffmann School Day Camp players, bees, flowers, etc., in the persons of tiny human beings. We went on to luncheon at a little Hudson Riverside restaurant, Roxy's Lighthouse, in Yonkers, where sitting at the water's edge the small sail made Elwyn nostalgic for his youth in Wales. We had much excitement in preparing for a forty-person party we gave to Elwyn at my home in the evening; Elwyn and I decided to dress formally, his white jacket most resplendent, and then a few others arrived in dinner jackets, John Amos, my friend and client, and Luis Garcia, his informally adopted son, among them. They were flown up from Columbus, Georgia, together with John's wife, Elena, in the company Hansa jet and with them the company photographer. He was everywhere seen taking pictures on the promise that he would destroy the negatives. The heroine, planner, organizer, inviter, caretaker, for all this was, of course, my wife Anna. The affair catered by Babbington seemed extremely beautiful with dinner at little white tables on our terrace, each with a panoply of flowers, but it was marred by a drunken federal judge who arrived sodden and departed in the same condition and succeeded in making a nuisance of himself by insulting some of the ladies and uttering incoherent speeches. Lord Elwyn was his gracious and witty self. I introduced him, making a special point of praising Morris Ernst, who was present, who then was 86 years of age. I think we all had an excellent time. Sam Harris, a splendid lawyer, whom Elwyn knew from his Nuremburg prosecution days was among those present.

Saturday we loafed a good deal, swam, told jokes and autobiographical anecdotes. None of this was preserved on paper although some were salty British limericks as to which regrettably I failed to ask to be refreshed. His Lordship and I did much quoting, his concentrated more on parliamentary and barrister quips, mine on hortatory and Shakespearean verse. Elwyn sported an enormous, brocaded red robe bearing the Chinese good luck symbol, purchased by his daughter Jo in Hong Kong. It was resplendent enough even for a Lord Chancellor, and not without a suggestion of Poo-Bah in D'Oyle Carte's presentation of the "Mikado".

About 8 o'clock after a mix-up which brought the British Ambassador's car to my office at 12 East 41st Street, rather than to my home in Riverdale, we were picked up by the Embassy's Rolls Royce and driven to dinner at U.N. Ambassador Ivor and Lady Richard's. About a dozen guests were there including one McIntyre, Ambassador from Australia, Max Schreiber, Vivica Lindfors, the actress, and a lady with a beautifully bronzed back, who claimed she had the right to spend $28 million of Arab money to buy American real estate.

Ivor Richard, himself a Q.C., seemed to be a very bright and gifted representative of the U.K. Elwyn's charm, however, made the party most bearable and we were amused that the great Rolls Royce which called for us and returned us to Riverdale seemed to attract the attention of all passing cars, together with occasional comments which if they could be recalled would not be recorded here.

We arose early on Sunday, August 11, and packed our things for the Boston trip. I drove my car onto the pier next to the QE2 where we met Lady Polly arriving from England at about 9:30 in the morning. Polly thought flying was contrary to natural law. Once again the fact that Elwyn was the Lord Chancellor had considerable extra-jurisdictional effect, particularly on the personnel of the Cunard pier; without any untoward incident or delay we were able to whisk Polly off the boat and into the car. We then drove aimlessly around lower Manhattan and Greenwich Village for about an hour because Polly was eager to see the Village and we saw Polly off on the 11:00 A.M. Amtrak train going from Penn Station to Boston. His Lordship preferred seeing the countryside to traveling by train so they travelled separately. We returned to Riverdale where we stuffed Polly's things, as well as Elwyn's, into what our friends call the "boot" of the car and set forth to Boston. We had lunch later on at the Clam Box in Wethersfield, outside of Hartford where the distinction between Manhattan and New England Clam Chowder was plain. After a brief stop-off at the Davises with my daughter Jessica becoming our pilot, we arrived at Josephine and Francis Gladstone's[7] house somewhere around 6:00 P.M.

We dined with the Joneses at Josephine's house. We had some Gamy of Mondavi, a light-bodied California wine, I had brought along and which the Joneses were polite enough to say they liked very much.

On Monday, the 12th, his Lordship, having become ensconced in the Harvard Club in Boston, said he liked it very much because it resembled the House of Lords. I had luncheon with him and thereafter, we went by cab to Cambridge where I showed Elwyn the Harvard College ("Widener") library. We looked in the library index boxes for our books, and his and mine, such as they are, were all there. We walked across the Yard to Appleton Chapel. The Lord Chancellor was much impressed by the number of Harvard men who had died in World War II; their names are found in bronze on the walls of the chapel. He had four or five brief and informative chats with wondering students as he crossed the yard.

---

[7] Josephine (daughter of Polly and Elwyn) married to Francis Gladstone, great-great grandson of Prime Minister Gladstone.

We proceeded next to the Law School at Langdell Hall. We chatted with Paul Freund who pointed out that one of the things the Supreme Court did in the Nixon case was to create an executive privilege, albeit limited to security matters.

I had, before this, called President Bok's office where, to my amazement, Bok's secretary told me the President was busy in conference and I should take the Lord Chancellor to the Marshal's office where he might sign the guest register and someone there could be found who would show us around the Campus. It occurred to me that the Warden of one of the colleges of Oxford or Cambridge (Elwyn is a Cantabrigian) would have welcomed the arrival of Chief Justice Burger of the United States Supreme Court as if he were visiting royalty. Lord Goodman once gave me a note to Jack Sparks, Warden of All Soul's College, who grandly received Trudy and me at Oxford asking over Harvey's Bristol Cream that remarkable question concerning the contemporary Columbia University student sit-in, "Why aren't these young felons in jail"? The Lord Chancellor is a most important personage, presiding as he does over the House of Lords, the entire structure of courts, and appointing most of the United Kingdom judges. His powers include those of Chief Justice of the United States and, Vice-President of the United States presiding, as he does, over the House of Lords. But the young woman who served as secretary to the President of

Harvard University could not be expected to be all-wise, although she might have been expected to be cautious.

The Elwyn-Jones/Harvard episode reminds me that a friend, with his friend, was introduced to Leo Szilard and Albert Einstein (wearing a motheaten sweater) at a little restaurant in Princeton. After the introductions my friend's friend said, referring to the man in the sweater, "Would you mind repeating, I didn't catch the name."

Two days later we drove to New York City with my grandsons Joshua and Alex Davis, arriving at dinnertime to find the Union Jack and the Stars and Stripes still standing in a corner of the living room.

I have just reported from a contemporary note the details of the Joneses visit in August 1974, but this visit was not without preparation. As already noted, Lord Elwyn and Polly came separately to be guests in my house, Polly by the Queen Elizabeth II since she did not fly and Elwyn via British Airways. The impending visit of the Lord Chancellor caused considerable excitement in my home and I at once developed a concern about his safety which was perhaps somewhat exaggerated in face of no threats or even knowledge that the Lord Chancellor was on the way to this country.

On June 27, 1974, I wrote to Elwyn as follows:

I have talked with Francis and Jo concerning the problems relating to the safety of your person. I suppose you will travel incognito and with adequate protection. As soon as I learn the approximate time of your stay with us I shall engage a private security guard to stay in our house during your presence, unless, of course, you advise me that other arrangements for your security will be made. For example, if you are to be accompanied by a secret service man we can provide a place for him to sleep in the building. I know that Francis is writing you concerning these matters."

The plan was that after visiting with us in Riverdale, New York, he would stay at the Harvard Club in Boston while visiting his daughter and grandchildren who lived in nearby Brookline. There had been plastique explosions in London, for which the IRA had claimed credit, including one on Downing Street not far from the Prime Minister's residence. I was suddenly made sensible to the idea that housing the Lord Chancellor was a vast responsibility and so my letter went on:

If you are planning to stay at the Harvard Club in Boston, I urge you not to sign your true name there lest within one-half hour your presence is made known to the press. As you

probably know, Boston has a large Irish popu-
lation and the IRA is strong in Boston. As for
New York, unless otherwise instructed, I am
planning when you are with us not to let your
real person be known and to introduce you
around as a British barrister named "Smith",
"Jones" or, better still, "O'Sullivan".

Values are not always correctly discerned and
action is more unplanned than planned. The pre-
sumption of my concern was not quickly apparent
to me. The number two man in the British Government would certainly be tuned into danger if any
danger existed. There were no efforts made to
protect Elwyn as far as I could discern on his way
to the States. The day before he arrived a big black
Rolls with two distinctly M-4 looking types drove
into our ground slowly and without stopping turned
around and exited. I had the sense that this was a
scene from a John Le Carre spy drama. It was
possible to think that one of the men in the car
resembled Alec Guinness. FBI men they were not.
There were no double-breasted raincoats.

The next morning I met Elwyn at Kennedy Airport, congenial and apparently unfatigued by his
journey. I was called for by a black Rolls driven by
one of the two who had cased our place the day
before and the Lord Chancellor and I rode back in
this same vehicle to my home in Riverdale. It was
explained to me that there was no secret aspect to

the trip at all. The driver just wanted to know how to reach my house in advance so that he would make no false turns.

In my warning letter to Elwyn, I remarked with a sense of indignation that some young men of the IRA had slashed canvases at the British Museum. "I have never been quite able to make peace with senseless violence, though I believe I am tolerant as most with violence that has some demanding point."

I once represented the College of the City of New York in connection with its disciplinary hearing involving students who sought to block the progress of a bulldozer with their soft young flesh. This was 1969, and students everywhere were acting out in ecstasy the revolt sparked by Henry Marcusi at the University of California and "Red Cohn", the West German student who excited the undergraduates of Germany and France.

And yet this was not altogether useless violence because out of it came important self-examination of university methods and aims, and out of it also came more intense recognition of the difficulties minorities have in meshing into a success-oriented society.

But the letter I hold in my hand now goes on:

> I sense from what Jo tells me how great your compassion is for all people in trouble, including the Irish whose senseless violence

now includes slashing by coin the paintings of Rubens. In a perspective of galactic values where man is seen located not too far away from the salamander, where civilization struggles slowly rising on the shoulders of one generation after another to peer only quizzically and for a little time down the vast canyons of space searching for cause and effect, in such a context as that, would one ignorant teenaged kid, quick to destroy, be worth a canvas by Rubens? The world has too few glories left in it; Rubens is one of them, but we vote for life over art. Perhaps, however, there is some cruel and unusual punishment which should be meted out to defacers of paintings. The garrison of Drogheda is being avenged by people who no longer remember it, nor, I think, why they fight but they cut canvas and bomb ancient Westminster Hall where Sir Thomas More stood trial as easily as downing a bottle of beer.

Obviously the first sentence of this quoted matter should have qualified the word Irish with Republican Army since any ethnic comment is foreign to my way of life. But there was no reason for any of my alarms. Our visit included many hours of friendly and philosophic exchanges, occasionally assisted by the presence of La Phroic, that wonderful single malt scotch which was peacefully absorbed by us.

The sense of humor of Elwyn was celebrated by American lawyers as well as Brits since on several occasions he addressed American audiences, and in 1976 the American Bar Association invited him, and he accepted, to address the national organization in its annual meeting that year in Atlanta, Georgia. The humor expressed at that meeting is legendary among lawyers who were present.

At the annual dinner, this charming Welshman upheld "the Welsh claim that America was not in fact discovered by Christopher Columbus but by Prince Madoc of Rhos-on-Sea". There the Welsh were supposed to have landed in Mobile Bay, and traces of their speech are said still to be found in certain Indian tribes.

Elwyn burst out in song much to the delight and amazement of the American lawyers, some of whose concept of poetry consists of well written devises to heirs and trustees. In his autobiography "In My Time" (p. 291), he claims that the American lawyers urged him to sing the song of the Welsh discovery of America and so he did:

> Behold on a fair morning
> Thirteen small ships set sail
> On a dangerous venture
> May God preserve them from wave to wave.

His Lordship "accepted the invitation of the American Bar Association . . . no doubt to raise a glass to George Washington and others whom my predecessors in office would have undoubtedly hanged." (Letter to MAH of 14 July, 1975.)

We decided to exchange tapes instead of letters, and, in aid of this project, I equipped his Lordship with a cassette player, tapes, etc. He hoped that the tapes would not be distorted by electronic anti-spying devices. He wrote:

"I remember having a forensic experience of tape-recording troubles when I defended one Aloysius Cristember in what used (because of its Scottish founders) to be called Blantyre in Malawi some years ago. He was charged with incitement to violence in a public speech. The press recorded it on a machine previously used to record Louis Armstrong playing the St. Louis Blues. Unfortunately that music had not been obliterated on the tape. When it was played as an Exhibit in Court, the bare footed African audience began to beat time with it with their feet. The Judge was a bit deaf and took no action til the wooden rafters of the Court began to shake. Unfortunately enough of Cristember's words did come through to establish his undoubted guilt." (Letter to MAH of 14 June, 1975.)

My friendship with Elwyn had started when he was head of our Chambers and had carried through his attorney generalship. I expressed a little uncertainty as to what it should be now that he had reached such eminence as the Lord Chancellorship. His true graciousness is reflected in his letter to me of May 14, 1974:

"Your comments about social dealings with the Lord Chancellor reminded me of the letter Lord Maugham (himself a future Lord Chancellor) wrote to Lord Buckmaster on his appointment as Lord Chancellor:
'Your post is one of almost absurd eminence, the sort of uncanny position that my instinct tells me no friend of mine ought to occupy.'
I am happy to tell you that my occupation of the post has not yet affected any of my friendships, least of all will it affect ours."

His dear wife and colleague, Polly, to whom he was devoted from the beginning of their marriage to death, proved also a great friend of ours. She stayed with us in Riverdale on occasions when her husband was in Europe and although her colorfulness bordered on eccentricity, that eccentricity was divine. Living in the Lord Chancellor's apartment in the House of Lords, she reported to us:

"I cracked a vertebrae but it is mending nicely. I slipped on some damn highly polished lino outside the bathroom and I cannot tell you with what speed the powers that be covered it all instantly with non-slip carpet. (They always take years to do anything here - they must have thought Elwyn was going to sue them). I never mind staying in bed, provided I can spread myself in great luxury with books and drawing materials and endless supplies of china tea ....

• • •

I do miss you both and your darling hospitable flat and especially the gorgeous, gorgeous floors. I find it such a happy and inspiring home to work in and work very well indeed for me. On the other hand this residence is exactly the opposite.- Floors are covered with a depressing ladylike coloured carpets and it is very unsympathetic. Indeed nothing at all creative is to be found in the House of Lords. I hope they don't send me to the tower for saying so."

The care given to the apartment of the Lord Chancellor was abominable. Detecting the odor of gas, I went into the kitchen one day and saw a hole almost as big as an American quarter on the side of a gas pipe leading to the burners on the range. I stuffed a towel into the hole and maintenance was summoned. The caretaker seemed not at all surprised by the difficulty, used his own towel for a more elaborate tourniquet and it took another day before the hole was filled by soldering. I do not know whether the ancient pipe was ever replaced.

This difficulty brings to mind the trouble of the woolsacks. The woolsack is a pillow from which all important decrees must be signed and on which the Lord Chancellor presides over the House of Lords. A duplicate is kept in the Lord Chancellor's apartment so that certain solemn rituals can be followed in case of disaster. A previous Lord Chancellor whom I shall not mention because of a proper respect for the basis on which he worked apparently suffered from disquieting irritations of his backside. Polly told me that the wife of the former unfortunate Lord Chancellor reasoned that since these woolsacks had probably not been cleaned for four or five hundred years, the fabric might have caused the trouble. Surreptitiously she had the woolsacks at different times taken from the House and thoroughly cleaned. It is regrettable, she reported to Polly that cleaning of the woolsacks in no way improved the Lord Chancellor's condition. Blessedly, these matters were of no concern to Elwyn.

The kitchen in the Lord Chancellor's apartment in the House of Lords was equipped with a large deep, old fashioned British sink and breadboard. I arrived at the apartment one morning in time for late breakfast which the Lord Chancellor cooked for me. He had hardly finished his work when a bell rang from the cabinet room below indicating there was some matter as to which his presence was required. He took the elevator down, promising to be back in as few minutes and was as good as his word. He sat for a few minutes longer and now we were at coffee and the bell rang again. I finished my coffee and said to myself something like the following: "If the Lord Chancellor makes breakfast for you, the least you can do in return is to wash the dishes." I thought a little of the possibility that Jones had learned to fry eggs in his hometown of Wales as a boy and it was certainly true that I, in my hometown of White Plains, New York, had learned how to wash the dishes. I started at this endeavor when the Lord Chancellor sprang into the kitchen again, freed once more from his official tasks. He protested loudly that I must not wash the dishes, this was part of his duty as a host. This was hardly a conversation which one might have expected Sir Edward Coke would have had with a lawyer or Sir Thomas More, the martyred Lord Chancellor. This was the Lord Chancellor who did dishes and almost everything else that was important in England.

Elwyn's politeness and gentility bespoke the true Welsh courtesy found in the homes of apprentices to tinsmiths rather than in royal palaces. He often referred to his father in a tone almost of reverence because it was his father who insisted that the children pull far above their semi-literate milltown backgrounds. All of them did with great distinction.

The entwinement of Polly and Elwyn cannot be unravelled since they seemed always to think approvingly of each other's projects and interests as if they were a single project although done in different fields by very different persons. For example, Polly was until her death writing plays, little snatches of thoughts, books about unusual people, and drawing and painting or making pottery or stage sets or artistic bric-a-brac. She was a small woman with the liveliest eyes in the world. She was loved by most but thought absurd by some. She sought to improve the condition of the "Pearlies", the Cockneys who elect their own rulers and have their own shadow government and are identified by the pearl buttons sewed on their clothes, for which mountains of buttons have been sent from Japan and other faraway places. She was the champion of the "poor and oppressed" and the farthest thing from what might be expected of a Lord Chancellor's Lady.

Elwyn has described how he pursued the brilliant young reporter whose dispatches to the London Times about Russia in the 1930s, illustrated by her imaginative drawings, made him feel enchanted. They met in England, spent some time together in a friend's home in Venice where they were staying to revive their strength after separate illnesses. She was the daughter of a poor Jewish immigrant in Soho and their marriage, of apparently antipodal people, was in fact a fusion of great faith mellowed by skepticism. The faith was not in religion as it is customarily understood or in the rituals of the Christian religion or the Hebrew religion.

In 1967, as Lord Chancellor, Elwyn opened the law courts with a great celebration that accompanies this event each fall, including an entertainment of the leaders of the Bench and Bar, in the Prince of Wales Room in the House of Commons, and a party in his apartment given by his Lady for some of the wives of these dignitaries. Polly was absolutely regal that day. She had marched down Westminster aisle in a great green robe which swept the carpet. She wore a small green cloche with a modest tiara. Her manner and pace were majestic. I was a guest of the Lord Chancellor at his party while Anna was with Polly in their apartment. Polly had neglected refreshments or perhaps had decided against that, but she had a large bowl of peanuts.

The Joneses came back to New York soon again. Met Elwyn, and we at once drove to Riverdale where Elwyn established himself in his room which we had by that time dubbed the "Lord Chancellor's apartment", and then we had coffee and buns with Anna and exchanged pleasantries.

I drove Elwyn to the Petite Marmite on East 49th Street where he kept his luncheon appointment with Ivor Richards, the British Ambassador to the U.N.

Elwyn, after luncheon, was driven by the Embassy Rolls Royce to my office and announced that he caused considerable excitement among the young women of New York, either as a result of the Rolls Royce or his handsome Welsh features. In the interim an extraordinary event was experienced in my office. One of my partners, staring out the window of his room, noticed two men equipped with long-distance telescopic sighted rifles as well as a camera arranging their instruments on the roof-top south of us, not more than fifteen feet away. I called the police who quickly arrived, one of them saying as he looked out the window, "My God, it's for real". Another then went to my partner's room, opened the window, drew and cocked his revolver and said to a young, blonde man, "throw yourself on your belly with your hands outstretched and freeze." The young man did so and the police officer covered him with his revolver while other officers went to the roof of the building and took the equipment apart. One young police officer was seen peering down the barrel of the rifle and it is probable that the whole matter came to nought because we later saw the blonde young man picking things up off the roof. It probably was the case that the gun was unloaded and what we witnessed was some photographic stunt. The matter cannot be associated with the Lord Chancellor's presence because the miscreant's perch was not a vantage point which covered 41st Street from which Elwyn approached our building, nor my suite, except for the back windows. It could not win a dinner as an aborted attempt. He was most unhappy that he had missed the whole affair.

Elwyn wrote to me, "I was interested in your reference to Becker's book "Escape from Evil". I confess that I myself, up to now at any rate, have not been haunted by the fear of death nor am I conscious of a longing for immortality. It may be that these things creep on one with advancing age. It is a development which might be avoided by the solution of one of my friends who has retired to a quite seaside town in Wales - Pwllheli. I asked him why he had retired there and he said "Oh! in Pwllheli the transition from life to death will be hardly perceptible."

We had exchanged thoughts about writing autobiographies. Two publishers pressed Jones to do so and in 1983 his project was complete. I had already written a few pages and mentioned them to Elwyn Jones in 1974. He had no plans to undertake the project at that time, writing, "I am interested that you are working on an autobiography.

Two publishers here separately take me out to lunch once a year hoping to commit me to writing my memoirs. I continue to take their hospitality, warning them that I do so on false pretences, that I have no present intention of meeting their wishes either jointly or severally. ... you clearly have enough creativeness in you to produce "a book of ideas and insights". My predecessor, Lord Hailsham, has just produced such a book here, mostly related to his emergence from atheism into total belief in the Christian faith and the Church of England. I must say I enjoyed reading your book about your early career in public service and as you have a capacity which you should put to good use in this field, I hope you will persevere with your idea."

This is July 1994. Elwyn's "In My Time" was published, and Elwyn himself is gone. We had been friends in many relationships early on. His Lordship stepped up to the question as to whether the defendant might properly be convicted of assault when by reason of his self-induced intoxication, he was not able to intend the act alleged to constitute the assault. The Lord Chancellor considered that the issues raised were of very great public importance and decided that an Appellate Committee should be constituted with seven Law Lords to consider the problem. I was delighted that in one of his letters to me the Lord Chancellor described this event and asked me for some minor assistance. "I have no doubt that there is much American authority and academic learning in this field and if one of your young colleagues could direct me on to some of it, I would be very grateful. Just a reference and the names of one or two of the cases is all I want, but please do not let this request interfere with the considerable calls which I have no doubt they already have on their time in your busy practice."

There was some question raised by a well-known British law commentator, Francis Cowper, as to whether or not Elwyn Jones who had been Attorney General in the last Labor government should accept the peerage which went with his elevation to Lord Chancellor. Others who had become Attorney General and Solicitor General had refused to accept the knighthoods which customarily go with these titles. Not Elwyn, who had no qualms about accepting his barony in 1974. It was obvious that the Labor Party of the United Kingdom would not seek to bring down the monarchy or the institutions of the Peerage. I responded to Cowper with a letter to the New York Law Journal in which I said: "If members of the Labor party were expected to bring down the monarchy and disassociate themselves from the last of the intricate symbolism which makes up British formal life you can be sure that the Labor Party would soon become foreign to the spirit of Britain and probably could not obtain office." Elwyn pointed out in a letter to me that a contemporary Lord Chancellor "has to be a Member of the House of Lords and therefore a Life Baron (or of course a hereditary one). This is because he is a Member of the Cabinet and a senior Cabinet Minister representing the Government in the House of Lords. As such he has to take an active part in debate on the Government's policy and activities and in steering Government Bills through the House of Lords."

Elwyn visited the prairie provinces of Canada. He was given an honorary Doctor of Laws by Ottawa University and participated in several symposia in different parts of Canada concerning the role of Appellate Courts. I mention it only because it gives rise to the testimony of J. B. Johnson, the British High Commissioner in Ottawa: "Jones' trip was a notable plus for Britain with ripples spreading far outside the fraternity".

Violence on the streets of London and other difficulties in keeping that city together caused "problems of government which we are now battling in all too frequent Cabinet meetings. Some are taking place out in the Prime Minister's delightful residence at Chequers in the country. A beautiful house of the Tudor Period full of history including the incarceration there of one of the many trouble causing royals of the sixteenth century."

The presence of the Joneses in the States in connection with the glorification of the Magna Carta which involved presenting the Congress with a true copy amidst much ceremony in which Elwyn Jones wore his Lord Chancellorship robes, perhaps for the only time they had been worn in Washington, D.C. We made plans for the supplementation of his trip to Washington and our correspondence caused Elwyn to comment about Magna Carta in a way which shows how true a realist he was and how little seduced as to words as opposed to their meaning: "The interesting historical feature about Magna Carta is that King John, having got his undertakings withdrawn by the plea that they were given at Runnymede under duress, Magna Carta seems to have disappeared from the scene until Sir Edward Coke revived it in the fight against the Crown in the 17th century. Shakespeare did not mention Magna Carta at all in his historical plays. Oliver Cromwell's vulgar commentary on Magna Carta was "Magna Carta! Magna farta", a commentary which I feel it would be inappropriate for me to mention at the joint meeting of the U.S. Congress and Senate!"

Elwyn-Jones was eight or nine years older than I. Polly a few years older than Elwyn. Our friendship was cemented while we were well on in middle age or in "late youth" under my method of measuring life. That measurement is to divide the lifespan into three: "youth", "late youth" and "how well you look". It is not easy for people to make new friendships as they go past the age of desire for power or aggrandizement. In a sense I think friendships of the elders have more cement in them because there is less need for advantage and more need for the banishment of loneliness.

Elwyn and Polly remained close to their children and immediate family, as indeed did I. The result of these comparatively new friendships was that the next generation, Jo and Francis Gladstone daughter and son-in-law of the Joneses, and Will and Jessica Davis, my son-in-law and daughter, increasingly spent time with each other and shared life experiences.

For an extended time the Gladstones lived in the States, where Elwyn Gladstone II was born. His brothers and sisters went to American schools, but he is the youngest. He became a pure English schoolboy upon the Gladstones' return to England.

I accompanied Elwyn to Brookline when he was first introduced to his new borne grandson. I had written to him earlier that this boy, under our Constitution, could become President of the United States, to which Elwyn replied that he had a very different intention for him. I represented Francis and Jo in some legal matters in this country and we seemed in fact to be "extended families", in Polly's phrase.

I just missed seeing Elwyn in London prior to his death in November, 1989. Elwyn was leaving his home in Brighton to participate with the Queen in a public event in London and told me he only wanted to find the strength to perform this function. I had an airplane ticket for the following morning and thought it necessary to return to New York. My failure to see Elwyn was just as preclusive as my failure to go to see Bonnell Phillips on Thursday when he died on Friday. Elwyn did attend, travelling to London in repudiation of medical guidance, and he died a few days later upon his return to Brighton. Polly died not long after, perhaps ignorant that Elwyn had gone. Jo asked me to stand beside her at the memorial service at Westminster and read with her from the common prayer book. I did not go.

The Service of Thanksgiving for the life and work of Frederick Elwyn Jones took place at Westminster Abbey on February 8, 1990 and nothing could have been more appropriately planned. The 23rd Psalm was sung, although slightly altered from the work of King David so that it now included a reference to the Father, Son and Holy Ghost. Next followed a reading by Dr. Lionel Kopelowitz, President of the Board of Deputies of British Jews, from the short, wonderful Book of Micah, "And what the Lord doth require of thee: Only to do justly and to love mercy, and to walk humbly with thy God."

The great kings of England now fittingly looked down from their statues at the ceremony in Westminster Abbey in which a Jewish rabbi had participated, and the address was given by Michael Foot, a leader of the Labor Party and vigorous opponent of the traditional English as represented by its services at Westminster Abbey.

No mention, of course, was made of the fact that Polly was Jewish or Elwyn skeptical. Rather, the preacher to Gray's Inn said, "We remember the pride that Elwyn had in the home from which he came and the love of Elwyn and Polly for their family and grandchildren, and pray for the family life of our land." The bells of Abbey Church rang.

For a professional to reach high office in this country it seems to me he must become a public man; that is to say, he must speak and act with a small fire burning among the embers of his head, asking the questions "How will this look?", "What will they think of this?" If political battle becomes intense, as it does every four years for Presidential elections in this country, the candidate is no longer a gentleman. The stakes are high and it may be a crude rule of measurement that the higher the stakes, the lower the gentility. This observation applies today with such, force that manners seem to have disappeared, that personal life becomes public life, that indiscretions between the sexes govern campaigns, that a man's qualifications for the President may ultimately be decided by how indiscreet he was long before he thought of running for the Presidential office. Yet the Presidents themselves from the perspective of snooping journalists after the election may go into a catalog collected by a latter day Kraft-Ebbing listing aberrant sexual behavior.

The prim Woodrow Wilson had a great passion for Edith Bolling Galt, whom he married in 1915. He called her his "other self". Calvin Coolidge came soon, the laconic New Englander; if Coolidge had any love affairs it was consistent with his personality not to talk about them. Indeed, it will be recalled that he once went to church and was asked about the sermon preached by the local minister. "He spoke about sin" said Coolidge. The reporter was not exactly put off. "What did he say about it?" he asked. Coolidge gave his characteristic reply "He was ag'in it."

Now Coolidge was succeeded by Warren G. Harding in the days long before television. Harding was a rather lazy man who became the nominee out of the exhaustion of the convention delegates who finding their candidates unable to obtain the majority, settled upon Harding who had been the publisher of a small town newspaper in Ohio and had a very handsome profile which lent itself to suggestions of small town stability and propriety. It turned out that his administration was riddled with corruption. The Attorney General and other cabinet members were in on it, but Harding himself was not suspected because by this time it was generally believed that he didn't know very much about what was going on in Washington. A young woman wrote a book in which she claimed that Harding was the father of an illegitimate child conceived in the White House. It is said that Harding once approached the room clerk at the Occidental Hotel on Pennsylvania Avenue, only a block or two away from the White House with a young woman on his arm and sought to register as Mr. and Mrs. John Doe. The clerk refused to accept the registration saying, "I don't think you want to do this, Mr. President". Generally the American people learned about infidelity and other sexual activity after election time —but not before.

FDR, the glorious president who fashioned our welfare system and did more than anyone else to win the most important war of the century was paralyzed from the waist down. Occasionally there were rumors concerning a mistress whom he kept in the East 60s in Manhattan. So revolting was the idea that it was generally laughed away as a crude impossibility. After his death, taking place in the arms of his mistress in Hot Springs, Georgia, we learned that the truth was otherwise, but we did not falter in our admiration for this great man.

Harry Truman, who some think was the greatest of our presidents was a man of extraordinary strength of mind and vigor. Yet, I have never heard a suggestion made that he was in any way unfaithful to Bess, neither before, during, or after the Presidency.

Not so, however, with Dwight Eisenhower, the great war hero who was much admired for his integrity. He left a little lady behind in London after his stay there as Commander-in-Chief of the armed forces for the allied countries, and we didn't learn about it until after Ike became President. Ike, however, was not known for promiscuity and one can well understand the lonely position of a man with vast responsibilities functioning from headquarters thousands of miles away from home.

Along came Jack Kennedy, flamboyant, imaginative, cultured and able to understand and rely upon the advice of scholars. It was said that no woman was safe in the White House while Jack Kennedy was loose and his indiscretions became world famous allegedly including great movie stars and the like. Reflections about Jack Kennedy and the sexual habits of his brother, Bob, did not surface until after their assassinations. The Kennedys, of course, seem to have made of extramarital sex a family tradition.

Everyone seems to agree that Lyndon Johnson had moral failings aplenty. They were mostly along the line of servicing his fight to the top of American politics. But in the progress of his political life a poor country boy became very wealthy and with his wife owned television stations and other important assets not ordinarily found among hardworking politicians.

Unlike Harry Truman who in his one business adventure, a haberdashery in Missouri, went bankrupt, Lyndon Johnson seemed to succeed in almost every direction. Although his ambivalence toward the Vietnam War resulted in the meaningless death of many young men, it was he more than any other President, with the possible exception of Abraham Lincoln, who brought freedom to the black race in this country.

Now this grizzly chronicle is certainly unnecessary to my consideration of the gentility of the British, but that does not deter me. It may be pointed out that President Nixon when under fire startled the nation by his statement, "I am no crook", perhaps, suggesting that if he was not a crook he was something even more reprehensible. Later he was forced to leave the Presidency in lieu of being impeached by his brethren in the U.S. Senate. Still, I don't remember reading that he was in any way unfaithful to his wife, Pat, who was said to have been called "Pat" because she was born on St. Patrick's Day, although the Democratic Advocate later pointed out that she was not.

No one expected Reagan to behave because he had been for many years a movie star, and certainly that circumstance suggested that our handsome President remained popular with the ladies. I must state, however, that I have not read about any infidelities in the White House when Reagan was there. But I confess I have not read any of the biographies describing this period in Reagan's life. If there is a Bush scandal, I should have heard about it in 1992 during Bush's presidential campaign. I did not. As for President Clinton, my candidate, may the Lord bless him and keep him from harm.

This digression takes us far from the Brits who had their own scandals, but did so at the expense of their public lives when the scandals became known.

In November 1975, the House of Lords debated the Labor Relations Bill. My friends, Lords Goodman and Jones, were in that debate and clashed in a gentle way. I reprint from the report of the proceedings of the House of Lords on November 3, 1975, where contentions were made as to whether broadcasting as well as newspapers were to be included in a reform bill relating to freedom of the press. The bill before the House left an opening which might exclude broadcasting from its operation. To this Arnold Goodman, representing the broadcasters, submitted an amendment to make certain that it would.

> Lord Goodman: My Lords, might I ask the noble and learned Lord whether he could tell us by whom the field of operation is to be defined.

> The Lord Chancellor: My Lords, it will be defined by those who will be preparing the charter. They are the master of it; they will control it, they will determine.

Lord Goodman: My Lords, is it really being suggested that the question whether or not broadcasting comes within the ambit of the charter will be the responsibility of those people negotiating the charter within the newspaper industry? If so, it seems to me an astonishing proposition.

The Lord Chancellor: My Lords, the charter will be prepared by both sides of the industry. I am afraid I may not be getting the point which is in the wise head of the noble Lord, and if so I apologize.

These are two Queen Counsels and Lords debating an important issue with voices soft as lutes and gentility as fine as it has ever been in The House of Lords.

Lord Arnold Goodman
Eminence Grisè

I am writing about Lord Arnold Goodman, the London solicitor, my friend for over thirty years, and my impressions of him tinged by affection. This is not an entry for an encyclopedia of great men, but a record of friendship.

A precise description in words of the large head of Arnold Goodman perhaps needs a skill better than mine. It has already been drawn by the great British portraitist, Lucien Freud. Since Arnold's face lends bravura color to his words I shall, however, try my hand at detailing it. His hair is curly and generally cut straight above the ear. It was dark for most of the three decades I knew him and it is not pure white even now. It has thinned some serving more to outline his face in the manner of a Dutch Master's portrait. His forehead has numerous parallel lines deepening towards the nose but suggesting a developed power of thought control. It is as if the corrugations coordinate with the eyes extruding will and purposefulness. The face is very full and double-chinned. There are four or five moles along the break of skin next to the nose and perhaps a few others elsewhere. These are not unpleasant. Nor is the somewhat large and protuberant lower lip. All fall in line with the large eyes that help place emotion onto his face. The eyes give their own messages like "you may think that you can't and I may agree and yet I think that you should take my messages seriously". There is lively action between brain and voice. His wit is remarkably quick and sometimes so close to the precipitant that it passes slower minds without chance to register. It may cause a late chuckle as it filters through his audience. This means often that a second sally as sharp as the first is missed entirely. His lordship is sardonic, often whimsical, and he shows a striking ability to cut through the oleomargarine and get to the bread of the matter.

Over the years Goodman became, and it shows, an eminence grisè; his face and powerful frame transmit authority as though his wisdom had in some extraordinary way become wedded to his body. His inflections and swiftness of tongue seem also to speak for his massive frame. A debate with Goodman requires courage and the ability to accept put down without shame or grief. On many subjects his opinions are powerful and precise. He rarely scrapes along the edges of an idea like a carpenter with a plane. Nor is he a tacker. Generally his opinions are on the side of the angels but, of course, not always, and certainly not when he disagrees with me.

He is an Englishman to the core and a devout supporter of the Jewish people. I recall, in June of 1973, an evening was arranged at which Arnold was the guest of honor at a festivity of the Friends of Akim, the Israel Association for mentally handicapped children. Arnold arranged for Alberto Semprini, a non-Jewish, Anglo-Italian and a famous pianist, to conduct a concert for the benefit of those unfortunate children. I remember, this splendid artist lived in a houseboat, was immensely popular, and his program that evening included the "Rhapsody in Blue" and the "Arkansas Traveller", among a dozen selections, perhaps in recognition of the presence of Americans. The result of Arnold's presence and the cooperation of Semprini was to raise a sizeable sum for this organization which theretofore I did not know existed or had reason to exist.

He took me to the funeral of the wife of a very close friend. Present, among others, were some of the most eminent British Jews in politics and the professions. Yet the service was held in a tiny chapel on the burial grounds compelling most of the guests to be standees. There was little or no grass anywhere in sight. Large flat stone areas housed the dead. Goodman explained to me that this Jewish cemetery to which we had driven perhaps 30 kilometers from his home in London was the only Jewish burial ground available in that part of England. For a long time it had been prohibited to sell property for use as Jewish cemeteries and, indeed, there were restrictions against it in many existing land deeds. So, said Arnold, letting the facts speak for themselves, there are 600 or 700 years of bodies in this cemetery with no room to turn around.

His grand intelligence has caused him to be a solicitor for the Queen and others in the royal family and for several Prime Ministers. R. W. Apple in the New *York Times* called him "perhaps Britain's leading attorney". We know that if Goodman is brought into a matter it is of great seriousness or importance and I think he plays a part in British life unparalleled by any lawyer in this country. He is not a company man, not a bar association leader; not a senior partner in a big law firm where the partners and employees can help push the senior ahead. His little island and 60 million people have proved wise enough to reward genius for its own sake.

Once, soon after he was made a peer, I sat in Arnold's flat watching him tenderly open a crimson, silk case. In it was a parchment page in old English script designating Arnold Goodman as Baron of Westminster with all the rights and privileges there set forth. He had been made by the

Queen a life-time Baron, a member of the House of Lords, a reward earned in part for setting in motion the triumphant London Arts Council which revitalized the Arts in England. Arnold looked at me shyly — "not bad for a Jewish boy whose father was a shopkeeper in So Ho", he said fondly closing the case.

One August morning near the end of the Labor government under Prime Minister Harold Wilson, I received a telephone call from Arnold saying "there is going to be a small meeting in my honor a few days from now and I have to make a speech. I want you there. I would like you to bring a good joke or two from America for me. The place is the Waldorf Hotel. Meet me there at 6 o'clock, Tuesday. It is a meeting in my honor presented by the Counselor Law Society." I was overjoyed that Arnold had invited me, overjoyed that my affairs were such that I could at once comply without any real disarray to my law practice. I arrived at my hotel about two hours before the scheduled meeting. I phoned to Arnold who said there would be cocktails about 6 p.m. and that I should meet Sir Max Aitken who would take care of me, and I should tell Max that Arnold, the guest of honor, would be a little late. I began to be a little awed by my surroundings and some of the leading personalities of the British government. I was, after all a non-political American lawyer whose principal use for a dinner jacket was weddings, anniversary parties and New Year's Eve. Now I had a little trouble when this meeting took place not from jet lag nor the sundry forms of middle age malaise. When I checked into the Savoy I was full of excitement for the oncoming event and didn't notice that my intestinal tract seemed to be quivering like a harp with a bad string. Arnold, of course, was as good as his word. When I arrived, a clean cut young member of the British Foreign Service, Sir Max Aitken found me, because of my 6' 6 height, or perhaps because of my quaint Brooks Brothers clothing, and said he was Arnold's emissary and offered me a scotch and water.

There I was surrounded by several hundred government lawyers who were gathered to honor Arnold, and already had active glasses, Sir Max Aitken set out and found Harold Wilson, then Prime Minister, who shook my hand and the three of us each had scotch and water. We chatted pleasantly about aviation, the Savoy and other things which had little content, but my harp string quivered. Although I had majored in English literature at Harvard, this training hardly put me at ease with the Prime Minister.

Finally, Arnold arrived, grabbed me by the arm, and took me to the banquet room where loomed a huge dais. In the seating at the centerpoint was the Prime Minister, with Arnold to the left of him and I to the right of Arnold. To my right Lady Wilson, followed by Lady Polly Jones, whom I had not yet met but who would later play, along with her husband Lord Elwyn Jones and their children Josephine and Francis, an important part in my life. Indeed, I had hardly been seated when Polly leaned over the intervening guests and berated me for America having brought "Oh Calcutta" to London, a show which she felt was particularly obscene but which I had not even seen. She explained to me that some of the great ladies of London were writing letters to the *London Times* indicating indignation about the content of this musical, which apparently showed a good deal of nudity and perhaps a lot of imperfections. She felt torn about what she was doing. She pointed out that it was not censorship and that probably the ladies would have no great influence on the situation. This, I think, proved to be the fact. Now the Prime Minister rose and made a most delightful speech extolling Arnold and Arnold's wit and his great contribution to the United Kingdom. Now Arnold leaned towards me and whispered "Well?".

I was flabbergasted. I came without jokes. I had thought of a few witticisms at 35,000 feet on my way to Heathrow. They had flown away from me. The best I could do was to mumble into Arnold's ear Mark Twain's story about how when Gus died, there was little good to be said for him and his acquaintances gathered around the pot bellied stove in the center of the store trying to think of some way of doing homage to the dear departed.

Finally one of them said, "Gus was the best speller in the 6th grade." Arnold shrugged that one off and soon he was called on to rise. He started his remarks by passing reference to me whom he had imported 3,000 miles in order to give him a humorous story since he was deficient in this department. From then on he spoke without notes for perhaps 30-40 minutes amid gales of laughter which punctuated almost every sentence. He was a highly civilized and, indeed, eloquent Al Jolson. He spoke to almost unremitting applause. At this time the broken harpstring in my abdomen was twanging, warning me that I was after all a simple American boy.

Presently dinner was over, my face was chalk and my spastic colon was twitching to the tune of "Yankee Doodle".

The Goodman memories float together and create a sense of warmth and sensitivity even now as I dictate about him. British gentles would be unwilling or slow to write about their living friends, and I would not write about Arnold were there any possible suggestion that I consider him less than Olympian.

Year in and year out I sent my friends to this great man in England and with unfailing courtesy he called them at their hotels, often dined with them and gave them a sense of being welcome in his community. To some extent, I had insensitively dealt with Arnold Goodman as if he was a public utility, available to fill the demands of strangers.

Once my wife and I were in London dining with Lord Goodman and some of his friends. We were going on to Rome where we had reserved space at the Excelsior Hotel overlooking the Via Veneto. We discussed with Goodman and his friends worthwhile restaurants and the visual wonders of Rome, where we would stay for about four days while we were enroute to Naples, where I had a law matter to service. My wife and I strolled along the Via Veneto across the street from the hotel during our first morning in Rome. There we beheld the enormous bulk of Arnold Goodman peering into a window of a toy shop. It seems on impulse Arnold and several of the dinner companions of two nights before had reached a decision that a few days in Rome was an immediately appropriate holiday.

Thus, we dined again, this time in a restaurant deep below the surface of the city, in part of what once was an ancient Roman theatre and where the quality of the pasta exceeded even that to be found in the great Italian restaurants of New York.

We had a great friend together. Arnold Goodman admired Morris Ernst as much as I did and never failed to see Morris when he came to New York, even on a very brief business visit. Many a time Morris and I would have breakfast with Arnold in his rooms at the Pierre on a Sunday morning because Arnold was otherwise spoken for during the few days allotted to an American business trip.

One summer, in the early 1970s Arnold came to New York and we were both eager to visit Morris Ernst, who was then summering in his waterfront house on Nantucket Island, off the coast of Massachusetts. We flew to Logan field in Boston where we had a reservation to meet a small taxi aircraft which would carry us the rest of the way to the island. By the time we reached Boston a heavy rainfall was in progress and the little plane declined to take off in the bad weather. We had no choice but to return to New York. Nevertheless, we first took a taxi and, in the pouring rain and without umbrella, I showed Arnold a little of Harvard Yard, and we even dropped in on a graduate student whose address Arnold had in Cambridge. This exploit took an hour or two, but the weather did not improve. Consequently we returned to New York via the unflappable Eastern Airlines Shuttle.

While we were in the air I told Arnold of the wonders of a New York delicatessen store that was much favored by Judge Samuel Rosenman, the advisor to FDR, and my onetime employer. I recounted that I had been with Rosenman on a matter in the Justice Department in Washington and when we were through it was lunchtime. The Judge asked if my hunger could survive until we returned to New York since he wanted to eat in a New York restaurant. I had momentary visions of Lutece or some great food station, but when we reached La Guardia the Judge jumped into a taxicab and said "The Madison Delicatessen, 86th and Madison Avenue." In the taxi he explained to me the great joy involved in eating a rolled beef sandwich at this delicatessen.

My tale gave Arnold Goodman a clue, so that when we arrived from Boston at a rainsoaked La Guardia, he suggested that we do the same since he had not experienced a good delicatessen in thirty years. In both instances I ate cornbeef and cabbage, while Goodman following Sam Rosenman, had a rolled beef sandwich. I write both episodes down as instances of how whimsy may reach even the digestive system.

Lord Goodman and I were once scheduled to have lunch with Sir Dingle Foot in Brighton on a pleasant Sunday in Spring. We got about half-way on the Brighton Road, when the traffic came to a complete stop and people began to leave their automobiles and sit on rails and tree stumps near the road. We were able to turn off the road to a tavern, which served a quite satisfactory lunch. Lord Goodman had called Dingle Foot to explain it was impossible for us to meet in Brighton. We had gone about half-way through our luncheon before it occurred to us that Dingle Foot might have joined us in the tavern because the half of the road leading from Brighton to London was empty while the half leading from London to Brighton was blocked. We were too late, but were reminded of the story of Friar Bacon who with his assistant, Friar Bungay, was conducting an experiment designed to summon up the devil. Bacon succumbed to sleepiness and asked his associate, Friar Bungay, to watch the window through which the devil would enter. Bungay himself nodded off, but heard a great voice say, "Time will be" "Time is here" "Time has passed". He opened his eyes to see the devil's tail as he left through the window.

Had I known enough when I was young to realize that I one day would be old, I would have kept a diary, faithfully entering each day's events, a kind of latter day Pepys thinking that every episode in my life, as distinct from the life of everyone else, was important. Only occasionally did I make a diary entry, perhaps one a decade; but I have found one for 11/7/68. It relates to Goody:

> "Had lunch today with General Edward Greenbaum in his new offices at 437 Madison Avenue, on the 35th Floor.
>
> "He asked why Nixon had won. I thought it was due to a lack of communication, a failure of the media to transfer the character of Nixon to the minds and hearts of the electorate. I thought that Nixon was an unliked candidate and would have vast difficulty as the result of his limitations in integrity and imagination, particularly when confronted with a hostile Congress.

"We talked of our friend Lord Goodman and the General remembered a meeting of artists on the Island of Georgia off the Malta Coast. It was attended by representatives of the arts from 40 countries and was presided over by Thornton Wilder, the American playwright. Mrs. Greenbaum, a sculptress, brought her husband there as a representative of American sculpture.

"Thornton Wilder learned by taking a trial poll that a resolution favoring American artists for a selection of the site for a future meeting would pass. Goodman counseled him not to make the motion, even although it would pass because it would also add to the dislike of Americans from many of the artists who would be disappointed in the result. Greenbaum was urged to balance the loss against the gain. The Americans did and the next meeting was scheduled for a small country inhabited by active painters.

It was this practical wisdom which figured large in Lord Goodman's judgment and with time caused him to be consulted by most everyone in trouble. Sometimes the generous application of his genius to these problems caused misunderstanding and false claims about him. In 1978 Jeremy Thorpe, the former Liberal Party leader, was charged with conspiracy and incitement to murder Peter Bessell.

Bessell acknowledged that he had written a dishonest letter concerning an alleged homosexual relationship between Mr. Thorpe and Norman Scott, a male model. Bessell stated that he had written the letter at the suggestion of Thorpe and Lord Goodman. Goodman stated, "the day I propose that sort of thing, I shall be led off to some mental institution". So strong was the Goodman reputation for integrity that no one believed Bessell and none of the duplicity connected with the Thorpe matter was attributed to Lord Goodman, whose reputation, in general, made the charge itself seem reprehensible. I think that in this country the danger is that if a suggestion of wrongdoing is made it rarely is thoroughly wiped away, and rarely by use of truth alone.

His "flat" as the British call it, is marked by stringent security devices. The fruit on the British table is often over the hill and Arnold Goodman's breakfast table is not an exception. There seems to be some thinking that British palates enjoy old fruit and regard it as more flavorable then younger delicacies. The beef on Arnold's table was much better, aided by a splendid cook. Once I sent Arnold for a birthday present an electric powered carving knife. He acknowledged the gift in sinister fashion, saying, "Do you realize that you have put two assistants in my kitchen out of work".

Although in many ways favored by his client Harold Wilson, the Labor Party Prime Minister, who made him a life peer in 1965, Arnold sits on the uncommitted bench in the House of Lords and in politics remains an independent with an intelligence addressed to the truth of the matter rather than the party. When Wilson went on, Lord Goodman was sought after by the Tory Prime Minister Heath and had no political identification which would have made this representation embarrassing either to him or the new Prime Minister.

I did not know Arnold in his various professional activities other than in the practice of law. In 1971 he was selected to go with Sir Alec Douglas-Home the Foreign Minister, to Rhodesia to see whether he could solve the unsolved problem of the United Kingdom's relationship with that restive country. According to reports, this may have been Goodman's one unsuccessful negotiation, since the proposals for greater opportunities and such were not what the natives required. For a short time it looked as if he and Sir Alec Douglas-Home had succeeded, but the real demands could not be met without British surrender.

He has a house in Oxford where he has been serving as Warden of University College. His reign as Chairman of the Arts Council in the 1960's is still remembered and sometimes is criticized because Goodman was said to be "fastidious" in his taste. His apartment in London reflects this taste. He has a number of 19th Century landscapes and still life paintings which show the most precise and excellent British painters' work. For a time he headed the Observer Newspaper trust and served the movie industry as distinguished counsel. In one of his main speeches in the House of Lords he introduced legislation designed to put an end to censorship before the allegedly censurable exhibition, a process known in the States as "prior restraint". Our courts had put a stop to this early in the 20th Century. Goodman approached the problem in his own wry fashion. He would spare the Lord Chamberlain the unpleasant job of seeing bad shows and reading bad books in advance of publication. He saw no reason for Lord Chamberlain to have to perform these onerous duties when the publication could take place with the publishers taking responsibility for the harm, if any, after the event.

His submission to the needs of his friends itself has been startling. My daughter and I went up to Oxford while Goodman was in London and he proceeded us with a letter to Jack Sparrow, the Warden of All Souls College, urging him to welcome us. The year was 1969 and as I came through the door of Sparrow's house he, himself a barrister, greeted me with the question "How can you explain the fact that those young felons at Columbia University are still at large?" I responded by informing him that a registration card in the Columbia School of General Studies was a license to commit crime, such as kidnapping the Dean. He told me that the Oxonians sometimes peacefully marched down High Street singing songs of the impending Communist revolution, but always breaking up at 4 p.m., time for high tea.

I have been with Arnold and without him in his box at Covent Garden and observed the uniform respect and affection in which he is held. I have seen him greeted by the Duchess of Kent in most friendly fashion. His walk through the theatre is a royal procession.

Goodman is an enormous man about 6'4" and for much of his life carrying more stones than can be counted. He had 23 consecutive Rovers, a car which had a generous design for the front seat, making it possible for Lord Goodman to drive the car himself, a pleasure not available in other automobiles. He crossed the ocean in a Concorde for his client BEA and it was necessary for him to occupy two seats in order to enjoy this speedy trip.

In more recent years, however, Arnold Goodman purchased a Daimler because the Rover discontinued the large Sedan line and thereafter he gave up driving the car and used his own Rolls Royce equipped with chauffeur. I trust that the makers of the Rover who seem to be reviving the sale of the Land Rover will reestablish the large sedan for passengers of heroic size.

Arnold Goodman takes his responsibilities with seriousness and care that is, indeed, fastidious. Some years ago the 16 year old daughter of his departed friend and client, one of the wealthiest men in England, wished to come to the states for a visit staying with a young lady she had met in London whose father was a Professor in a northeastern university. What ensued was a careful scrutiny which would have done British intelligence proud. I was asked to inquire fully about the academic gentleman and did so. I found out about his teaching record at the university through friends and relatives. I learned about his reputation in the community. All this led to the conclusion that the young lady was part of a very respected family and a fine representative of American young womanhood. Arnold now approved his ward coming to the states. She stayed for a short time with me at my house and then went to New England from which she soon returned saying she was bored and wanted to go to the West Coast. Again, there were frenzied telephone conversations and letters between Goodman and myself while I arranged for her to travel to and stay with a family headed by a professor of psychology at the University of Southern California. After a stay of a week or so there, also by pre-arrangement, she was sent on to a friend in San Francisco who was a distinguished lawyer. Then she returned to my home in Riverdale and thereafter back to London. All with a flurry of letters and calls. She was a beautiful young woman and after her departure I learned she had broken two hearts— (1) of the professor of psychology, whose marriage was dissolved not long after, and (2) of a young man in San Francisco who fortunately soon was able to recover from the allied invasion. She capped off her relations with me by one day telling me that the whole apartment which we had in Riverdale on the top floor of a schoolhouse could be placed in the livingroom of her house in Mayfair with plenty of space left over. Goodman perhaps now is learning the details for the first time and I trust he is not dismayed. Our mission was accomplished.

Through Goodman I have met some of the great ladies and gentlemen of the United Kingdom, mostly by dining with them and Lord Goodman either in his apartment or in one or another of his favorite restaurants, such as "L'Escargot". Arnold would pour drinks but not consume them. It was from Arnold that I learned words like "orange squash" or lemon squash, which in this country used to be known as orangeade and lemonade, drinks which largely have disappeared since they are little more than flavored water. Arnold never smoked but I have lived in the time when his livingroom was full of smoke as was almost every gathering point in America. There is none now, not even in the conference room of my law office where lawyers gather and heed the Surgeon General's warning .

Arnold Goodman needs no award from me. We are both now octogenarians and perhaps we are a little slower than we were 35 years ago when we first met, but we live now, and there is much that society may still expect from his Lordship.

* * * * * * * *

It has been my good fortune to enjoy the friend-ship of the various heads of Chambers in the Lamb Building in the Temple, including Peter Downe, Lord Elwyn Jones, J. W. Priest, Sir Robin Auld and Michael Burke-Gaffney. The quality of these bar-risters has been evidenced in many striking ways by elevation of Jones to the Lord Chancellorship, Sam Silkin to the Attorney Generalship, and Sir Robin Auld, among others, to the bench. Sir Robin's extraordinary responsibilities, included represent-ing the Crown in international disputes in determi-nation of rights in Shanghai after independence, and in arbitral proceedings concerning nuclear testing in Australia.

From Michael Burke-Gaffney I learned much of England as practiced by English gentlemen. I did not know, for example, that cricket was a game in which many rotund persons in their 50s still delight, differing from baseball significantly in its relaxed qualities and the lesser quantum of activity imposed on each player. White trousers are essen-tial for the play and the fact that they are full length belies the need for any great speed in action. Michael Burke-Gaffney is a barrister whom I be-lieve does not exercise more often than during the occasional eclipse of the moon over the British Islands. But I watched him with cricket bat in hand stand at the plate opposed by a ferocious enemy in a game in which none of the players was under the age of 35 years and Michael hit with the eclat of someone who knew what he was doing, running back and forth without any apparent sense of the danger of instant demise. The Lamb Building's opponent was another chamber of barristers headed by a lord of fabled ability in playing this game. He was not a week under 65. Watching the play on a languorous Saturday afternoon, at a club near London, I was reminded of and forced to tell the story of the two U.S. middle aged devotees of softball, who played their game almost whenever weather permitted. They made a pact together that the first one who died would bend all his ghostly energies in an effort to inform the survivor whether or not baseball was played in heaven. One died and the other soon thereafter heard in his ear his friend's voice saying, "They sure do play baseball in Heaven." He gasped as the voice went on and said "What's more, you're pitching Friday."

* * * * * * * * *

At the emergence of the E.E.C., American law firms are opening branches everywhere, or making associations with existing firms in most capitals of the world. Certainly, these firms are destined to serve some real commercial advantage if lawyers are capable of receiving the input. It may also tend to level off concepts of substantive law in Europe and the United States. Such commonality will not easily be acheived, particularly as it relates to practice mixed with concepts of law. It is not easy for a lawyer in one state of the union to try a case in another, even though he is in the Federal Courts, where the concepts are much the same.

Trying cases in faraway court houses is often a difficult enterprise, as my own law practice demonstrates. I have in a long law practice been involved in judicial proceedings in Sweden, Denmark, the United Kingdom, Florida, California, Georgia, New Jersey, Pennsylvania, Massachusetts, New York, New Hampshire, Maine, Illinois, Ohio, Iowa, and Maryland. I may have left out a state or two and of course the bulk of my law practice was in New York. But it is Florida that I think about when searching for a jurisdiction where the law is not predictable and only brave men will enter certain courthouses. An old friend and colleague of mine brought an antitrust case from the plaintiff's point of view in Tampa, Florida. The friend was a well-known Washington lawyer. He succeeded in his case against most defendants but a banker and banking institution which were alleged to be conspirators in the offense were tried separately. He asked me to come from New York in order to testify as an antitrust expert as to the propriety of suing an officer as well as the company in which he officiated as part of the conspiracy with other companies. This frequently had happened in enforcement of the antitrust laws and I came to Florida so to testify against the argument that my friend's naming of these defendants showed that the lawsuit was brought in bad faith and was frivolous.

I brought my wife along for a short weekend holiday and I was called into the courtroom where a lawyer for my friend gave a long and laudatory introduction emphasizing all the achievements and talents which he thought I possessed. When he was finished, I took the stand and my testimony began. "What is your name?", asked the lawyer. I supplied it. "Where is your home?" I supplied that. "What do you do?" I told him that. "Where do you maintain your offices?" I told even that. Now there arose in the courtroom a very distinguished looking gentlemen with penz-nez glasses who represented the bank, and he made a speech as follows: "How does it happen that the great state of Florida does not have its own antitrust experts. How is it possible that the magnificent City of Tampa with its active court system doesn't have an antitrust expert? Can it be that present at this moment in one of the many parts of the court in this Courthouse there is not an antitrust expert? "The State of Florida", he exclaimed "is full of antitrust experts", and now looking at my client ominously and at me with great skepticism he said, "Why is it necessary for Mr. Rowley to go to New York to find an expert witness?" It seemed to me that he curled his lip as he mentioned "New York" and I did not like the expressions on the faces of some of the jurors as this speech was being made in open court.

From the bench there came a warning. "I don't think It necessary, Mr. Germane, for you to attack this witness." Mr. Rowley should never have depreciated our bar by bringing an expert from New York, and what's more I think that everyone in the courtroom should realize that Mr. Rowley, himself, the lawyer under attack in this case, is a lawyer from Washington, D.C. You may be excused, Mr. Hoffmann." I quickly left the courtroom and with my wife I was soon far away from it, swimming in the Gulf. My friend quickly followed since although he had brought a proper case he had found it necessary to make peace with his adversary by accepting the defense which had no basis in reality or law. My honorable friend achieved peace by an elaborate apology in open Court addressed to the banker.

On another occasion I was called into an automobile franchise case in Miami. Half a dozen Florida lawyers were already enmeshed in the case which involved the right to sell two important makes of cars in the Miami area. My client was a great local business man who was widely known. His lawyers were present for sundry reasons, some of which were incomprehensible. We talked through lunch and in a conference in court we decided to make a settlement offer. One of the lawyers of my client had been an Assistant District Attorney, and seemed to function with a sense of indignation because of my presence and the presence of the other lawyers on behalf of his client. All requested me to try to enmesh the Judge in a settlement negotiation. He had admitted me to practice in the case a few minutes before the noon recess as an out-of-state lawyer, saying ominously: "You'd better do things the way we do them here in Florida." The recess over, I noticed that my colleague, the former Assistant District Attorney, was no longer with us at counsel table. Presently the Judge took his station and I approached him to say that we had negotiations pending which might prosper if he participated in them. This, of course, was done with the consent of our adversary, but at the moment our former D.A. was nowhere to be seen. The Judge raised his voice with voracity, informed me that he thought what I proposed was totally out of order, although from the text of his remarks he did not seem to know what it was I had proposed. He muttered something about contempt of Court. He had those reddened cheeks which so often bespeak the lawyer whose staple for lunch is a martini with ice.

Later that day, with the intervention of the former D.A., and he seemed quite contented with himself, we were able to settle the case along the lines I was prepared to propse to the Judge.

Then we saw the Judge leaving the courthouse compound in what seemed to be a leftover Army jeep with a baliff sitting along side and carrying a shotgun on his knees. Local counsel explained that this Judge had been very active in some of the drug prosecutions in that area and lived in constant fear that a drug dealer was going to mow him down!

Similar justice is sometimes to be found in a courthouse in New York, although on the whole the United States District Court for the Southern District of New York maintains a high standard of judges. There are exceptions, of course, and when there is one, generally he is a mistake, and as the late Mayor of New York, Fiorello LaGuardia, said, "When I make a mistake, it's a beaut!" Mistakes, I suppose, are universal, and by no means confined to New York.

Once when I was young, I was called into a case in which two large "crispy pizza pie crust" machine manufacturing companies sued each other in Cook County, Illinois. I was asked to try the case because it included an antitrust issue having to do with an alleged illegal division of territories for sale of the product. Our client maintained his factory in New York; his cousin maintained his factory in Chicago. Occasionally, my client sold a patented machine capable of making "crispy pizza pie crusts." Illinois wanted its territory enforced in the states of Indiana, Ohio and Illinois, a territory reserved for the Illinois company. We wanted it set aside because this provision dividing territories was illegal. I was able to be admitted for purposes of the case through local counsel, a fine young lawyer, who as we climbed the courthouse steps said, "You know, there have been other disputes between these two families. This is the first one that has been settled in the courthouse." As I reflected on this remark, my knees began to make a loud knocking sound: in those days, one regarded Cook County, Illinois as the national seat of crime and thought of New York as a comparative model of Utopian behavior. I was not before the judge long when as to a point of evidence he hollered from the bench "that is hearsay". I said, "But your Honor, it falls under the shopbook rule as an exception to the hearsay rule". "It does not", said his Honor. I then defined the characteristics of the exception; statement had to be kept in the regular course of business and it had to be in the regular course of business to keep such statements. His Honor bellowed, "Don't give me any fancy exceptions to hearsay, this is hearsay - pure and simple." "I have known that", said he, "since I was in law school." Now the fire had come to my eyes, my legs were restless and my fighting stance set in. "I learned the shopbook rule differently when I was at *the Law School,*" said I, throwing all caution to the winds. My school was Harvard. This statement seemed to trouble him. With some gravity, he allowed the questioned document into evidence. Later I talked to my local counsel who liked the way I handled that argument, of which I was mindfully ashamed. He said, "*The* Law School" must have intimidated the Judge, since the Judge had gone to a night law school and by "The Law School", he probably thought I meant the day time program at the University of Southern Illinois.

I will end this dissertation on courthouses outside the City of New York with a tale told by Arnold Cutler in his book "The Art of Trial Tactics". A well-known lawyer had a case to try in a small town in upstate New York. He arrived the day before trial and inquired as to the existence of some young local lawyer whom he might engage as local counsel to sit at table with him and show the courtroom that he was not a foreigner. He was introduced to the judge by chance at dinner in the sole restaurant in the town, and this brash lawyer asked the judge if he knew such a person who might be prepared to sit at the courtroom table with him. The judge looking around to see if he was not being heard, said "My nephew is just starting the practice of law and I am sure he will be glad to join you". So it was arranged. When the New York lawyer called an important witness and was about to ask an important question, he turned to the young man at table and they chatted briefly. Subsequently, when he was cross examining at a critical stage, once more he broke his questions to chat briefly with the young lawyer. The jury came in with a very satisfactory verdict. Later his client who was present during these proceedings asked him how it was possible that so wise and experienced a lawyer would need the help of the young local lawyer in formulating questions. Our friend replied, "The first time I spoke with him, I asked, "Jim, are you married?" He said, "Yes". I asked, "Do you have any kids?" He said, "Three" The second time I spoke with him, I said, "How is your practice going? He said, "Just began". I said, "Hope you have great success." And the third time I asked him "etc., etc., etc."

Sir Robin Auld

In 1982 the Head of Chambers in the Lamb Building was Robin Auld, Q.C.. He is ruddy faced, square shouldered and with the sturdy build of a British oarsman. His chestnut hair is somewhat thinned on top, not sufficiently to call him bald, nor to say he should invoke some new therapeutic method to preserve it. "Somewhat thin" is an arrogant criticism which can only come from a much older man who having lost most everything else, still holds onto a thick crop of hair.

Robin became head of chambers in the Lamb Building and, of course, a Queens Counsel. He had a way of looking at you frontally which suggested that he was an honest man - how about you. When I first met him, we seemed to cut past all differences in background and life to find an instant basis for lasting friendship. His wife, Mary, is also a barris-ter, but for the first decade in which I knew the Aulds, she spent much of her time with two children, Tim and Rowan, both highly spirited English people of quality, with great hopes for high achievement. Latterly, now that the children are grown, Mary is deep in public service.

These children were raised in a remarkable country house called "Goldingtons", in a little hamlet, Sarratt, in Hertfordshire. Nothing could be more British than that address and nothing more lovely than the large house surrounded by the slow tipping green from the house through an enormous meadow. It is a subject for British landscape painting and in the 19th century it did not escape from this use by the brilliant green meadow painters. They were tuned into the beauty of earth forms and the majesty of flowers, which are everywhere in Goldingtons. It is said the British mystery writer, John LeCarre, was staying at a nearby pub at Sarratt when he discovered the house at Goldingtons and asked for permission to describe it. He then drew room plans precisely, almost to the inch; the details of the house later appeared as headquarters for British intelligence in his popular novel, "Tinker, Tailor, Soldier, Spy". Recently, it has served as the beautiful setting for the popular film, *Four Weddings and a Funeral.*When I first knew them, the Aulds lived in part of this huge country house which over the years they restored and now enjoy in its entirety. Today, Sir Robin Auld sits on the High Court, a much respected Judge and his wife, Mary among other public duties, acts as a Justice of the Peace.

Robin Auld was master of the Worshipful Company of Woolmen, an old guild with distinguished members, a few of whom haven't anything to do with sheep, but many of whom are decedents from ancestors who did. The Auld themselves, for a long time had sheep gamboling on their meadows.

Sir Robin Auld, like Peter Downe, Lord Jones and later Michael Burke-Gaffney, all heads of the Lamb Building Chambers had travelled so much for the Crown that they merited special rewards for travel as well as for their great skills. Peter Downe at the U.K.'s request, defended an accused traitor to the Crown during the revolution in Aden under circumstances where Peter had to be escorted by a soldier armed with a machine gun. The government insisted on Peter's taking this assignment and my recollection is that although it was a moment of armed hostility, Peter's client prevailed. Lord Jones served the Crown in much litigation outside of Britain, perhaps most notably during the Nuremberg trials in the prosecution of the Nazi war criminals. Michael Burke-Gaffney handled matters in the Middle East and in Hong Kong, but it was Robin Auld, in the prime of his practice as a barrister, who was called upon to defend Britain in an Australian inquiry taking place concerning the British experimentation during the 1940's of the atomic bomb in Australia.

There were numerous claims that atomic explosions incident to the government's experimentation had caused injury to native Australians. Thirty years later Robin Auld carried the delicate cause of British good will under cries of indignation and dreadful anger. During the inquest he conducted himself with such effectiveness that even the Australians acknowledged in print his fairness and skill.

Sir Robin, several times during the 1980s, represented Her Majesty in the change of sovereignty which will take place in the 1990s. We corresponded frequently and I showed Robin and his wife aspects of New York life not always seen by the traveling European. For example, we combined visits to the Hudson Valley with the Metropolitan Museum's demonstration of the Hudson River School of Painters, stuffy as that may sound. Along the river in Tarrytown, New York, the vistas from the New York side of the western shore are of an undeveloped hillside called the Palisades which was cut through into a steep incline by the Hudson River in its earlier days of turbulent strength. The views from the New York side are much the same as Washington Irving must have seen or Nathaniel Hawthorne who lived nearby, from their functional homes which have been preserved complete with butteries and saw mills. Robin and Mary delighted in locating the details of these 18th Century homes in the intense manner of an American tourist going through Westminster Abbey.

We had professional exchanges as friends. Robin in connection with proposed legislation called the Shops Act, investigated what the American experience had been with department stores offering their merchandise on weekends.

I was able to get information for him from the Chairman of the Board of New York's largest department store and learned that the most important reason for shops being open on weekends was that husbands and wives both hold jobs and their only times together to buy significant objects are weekends. Auld's report on Sunday trading caused one member of Parliament to accuse him of bringing about the end in England of Christianity as we know it.

I was able to assist him in perfecting his admission to the Bar of the State of New York.

His admission to the New York Bar reflects Robin's admiration of our court system more than any desire for personal advantage. Robin had to travel in mid-winter through heavy snow to Albany, the capital of New York State, on roads which were almost impassable. The lawyer assigned to question Robin for the State Character Committee fought his way through deep snow to discharge his function, but was surprised to find Robin at the appointed place and time. Robin had never seen Albany, New York, and indeed saw very little of it in finding his way from an airport considerably out of town as a result of the compassion of a brave car driver, who, after putting chains on his vehicle, battled the snow drifts to bring Robin safely to the Courthouse in Albany. Never have so many fought so hard to accomplish so little. The difficulty included the New York Bar's obsession with papers and certifications.

On December 3, 1983, Robin wrote:

"You were good enough to telephone about my much heralded but as yet unachieved admission to the New York State Bar. Within a day of your call, I heard from Chicago that a favourable report had been sent to Albany. That was the signal for another round of affidavits and certificates. Now it is only Ireland that is holding things up. The Inn of Court of Northern Ireland, in particular, is obviously having great difficulty in certifying that I have never been convicted of a felony in that troubled Province. I have had to leave for Hong Kong without sending the final application papers to Albany, but Jean will attend to it as soon as she hears from Belfast."

The snowy day described above was February 21, 1984.

* * * *

Robin was an enthusiast for the works of Ogden Nash. Although numerous, almost all were available in paperback, which I began to collect for the Auld family.

I managed to cross the Atlantic for Christmas parties and annual chambers parties conceived of and presided over by heads of chambers. Robin became one of the Directors of Kings College London and I the attorney for the Friends of Kings College London Association in New York, using my law offices for annual meetings and the like. This delightful association reflected Robin's friendship as did many other acts which suggested to me that the presence of the Atlantic Ocean as a barrier for the functioning of a friendship is not so big a deterrent as a thin partition between two offices.

I came to Merchants Hall, as Robin presided over a special meeting of the Worshipful Company of Woolmen, in dinner jacket, and would have worn tails if I had them, and sat at a dignitary's table when Robin presided over a formal meeting of British worthies to become the Master of the Worshipful Company of Woolmen. All present carried their honors in ribbons on their lapels, honors of all sorts, although I saw nothing from the 4-H Club. The representative of the Lord Mayor of London made a speech which was to be measured by the calendar and not by a watch. His droning blended well with the excellent Chablis and Bordelaise wine which accompanied different courses. Robin electrified the audience with his dry, quiet humour and powerful presence. He ended his remarks talking of his Irish grandfather who entertained his cronies with much reenforcement by Bushmill and other Irish liquor saying at the end with a graceful bow and the sweep of his hands "the doors are open and the moon is bright enough to show you your way home".

Presently the word came that Robin was appointed to the High Court and knighted by the Queen. Sir Robin continued his consuming devotion to the law, changing his address from Chambers to the Royal Courts of Justice, a move "across the road".

I take the liberty of quoting from a letter to me of January 16, 1988:

"The sadness at leaving Chambers was temporarily overlain by the quick start of my new job. I was sworn in by the Lord Chancellor at the House of Lords and by the Chief Justice in the Law Courts last Wednesday, and was immediately packed off on circuit to Birmingham for six weeks on the Wednesday evening. There, I live in some style in the Judges' Lodgings and am driven fully robed in a Daimler flanked with motor cycle outriders to court every day. My first case to try is one of conspiracy to murder, a gruesome exercise which is likely to take about three weeks.

You will be pleased to hear that I am allowed to come home at the weekend. That is a necessary antidote to the nonsense of the week. Lord Ackner called it "going from mink to sink".

When Robin reached the High Court we managed to see him in action and I observed that in his crimson robe he no longer appeared to be the strong willed barrister whom I had known, but had grown to a notable of England who might well have been the subject of a portrait hung on the courthouse wall in a large gilded frame. England seems to touch its functionaries with a proprietorship stamp of its own. These persons who reach positions mostly of respect and more of importance of function acquire with the office a cache which is probably taught by example but is never written down. Sir Robin was suddenly High Court Judge and his smile on the bench was judicial, not personal, and his politeness addressed to the Bar and to the litigants remained the same; although no one in private life can exceed the Aulds in such matters as sensitive and friendly understanding of other people.

I am so sensitized by my British friends that I tend to be favorably judgmental about them. In July 1985 Robin wrote "I am about the most unpopular man in Sidney (Australia) at the moment". Yet soon after he was praised by the Australian President for his statesman-like conduct of the British case at the Hearing concerning the nuclear experiments which terrified many Australians and did considerable damage to Australian property.

As the years rolled on, my trips to Europe were less frequent and I began relying on my British friends to seek me out in New York. Fortunately, as of 1994, this still is happening.

The difficulty in travel puts in mind the report to me of my old friend, Morris Ernst. His last solo trip was to London at age 84. He had already experienced several heart attacks and was aware in his case that, after a brief rest, he could once more go about his affairs. On this last trip, he had a very busy visiting schedule including many of his British friends. He stayed at the Dorchester and, when reading the paper in the lobby, felt one of his attacks coming on. He thought to himself that if he called for assistance, he would be taken to a British hospital for examination and might spend a week or two there, instead of visiting his friends. He said to himself that the prerogative of an old man is to sleep in an hotel lobby. He napped for an hour, then took himself to his room, showered, and thinking himself fit, went about his busy social schedule, returning a week or two later to New York with his heart attack just a brief memory.

* * * *

It is, of course, my privilege as a matter of age to be sententious, and yours as a matter of youth not to read my sentention. My cousin, Amy Bonner, a charming poetess, brought me to a meeting of the American Poetry Society. Present and talking was Robert Hillyer, whose collection of poetry had won him the Pulitzer Prize in 1933, and who was my teacher that same year. He read and criticized my stuff, using a friendly and imaginative mind. His collection included a poem called "Lullaby" which I recited to my girls in place of "Rock-a-bye Baby." It had splendid, stupefying lines like:

> The long canoe
> Towards the shadowy shore,
> One . . . two . . .
> Three . . . four . . .
> The paddle dips,
> Turns in the wake,
> Pauses, then
> Forward, again

I told Hillyer how this lullaby had conquered my daughters. He seemed overjoyed and volunteered to send me the manuscript page on which the Lullaby appeared.

There seems something more than a lullaby hidden in these words: The paddle dips, Turns in the wake....pauses, then Forward again," Is this not a summary of the human condition? If we can use Hillyer's poem as a mere ink scratch on a pad, perhaps it can be stretched into a critique of life. The "long canoe" is not just your canoe or my canoe, but it is this human community at the end of the Twentieth Century long canoe, from which all persons work paddles. "The shadowy shore" surely covers the unknown with its dark net. If the metaphor is life then we all paddle to an unknown objective. The long canoe is exceedingly important if you believe, as I do, that there is a commonality of human kind which changes and grows with collective knowledge and insight of generations. It pushes unceasingly forward toward the "shadowy shore" but it is a quality of the long canoe that it never reaches the shore.

I have read of an astonishing experiment. A small closed lake was stocked with bass. Fishermen threw in their lines with brilliantly colored lures. For a few days, the bass responded as if bent on suicide, grasping for the lures. After a while, only an occasional fish sought the lure, the rest which remained in the thousands would not even bite. Over time, there was some demonstration that the new generations of bass also would not bite at the lure. If this is an accurate description of an experiment done with integrity, then we learn that a group of living organisms, traditionally thought to be the lowest level of intellect, can learn from their environment and pass on this knowledge. If that is so, we stand high on a plateau of achievement which has changed our own consciousness as well as of the world around us. If that is so, we can one day hope to understand as we reach out and gather the farthermost stars. If that is so, we can one day hope to understand each other.